# Shou Zi Chew: Architect of the New Tech Era

## Micheal .E. Hunt

Shou Zi Chew: Architect of the New Tech Era

All right reserved. No part of this book publication may be reproduced, distributed or transmitted in any form or by any means, including photocopying, recording or other electronic or mechanical methods, without prior written permission of the publisher, except in the case of brief quotations embodied in critical reviews and certain other non commercial uses permitted by copyright laws

Copyright © 2024

# TABLE OF CONTENT

## INTRODUCTION

## CHAPTER 1: WHO IS SHOU ZI CHEW
### Childhood
### Academics

## CHAPTER 2: PROFESSIONAL JOURNEY
### Position at Xiaomi
### Significant breakthroughs and accomplishments
### Strategic objectives and vision
### Important programs and projects

## CHAPTER 3: INFLUENCE ON XIAOMI'S GROWTH

### Significant technological developments

### Strategy and Market Positioning

## CHAPTER 4: CHALLENGES AND CONTROVERSIES

### Major Decisions and Reactions

### Key components of Shou's leadership

## CHAPTER 5: PUBLIC AND INDUSTRY PERCEPTION
### Industry Opinions and Critiques

## CHAPTER 6: PERSONAL INSIGHT AND PHILOSOPHY
### personal convictions

## CHAPTER 7: FUTURE OUTLOOK
### Future Forecasts for the Technology Sector

## CONCLUSION

Shou Zi Chew: Architect of the New Tech Era

# INTRODUCTION

Few people have managed the chaos of the quickly changing technological scene with as much insight and vision as Shou Zi Chew. As the creator of the new tech era, Chew has actively influenced the digital environment in addition to adapting to it.

Under his leadership, the tech sector has experienced a turning point that has pushed innovation and redefined the limits of what is feasible. From his first forays into the business world to his important positions at well-known technological corporations, Shou Zi Chew has proven to be a remarkable trend-spotter, innovator, and leader of revolutionary teams. His path is evidence of his strategic vision and audacious decision-making, attributes that have made him a visionary in a field rife with volatility.

Shou Zi Chew: Architect of the New Tech Era

This book delves into the life and career of Shou Zi Chew, examining the ideas and methods that have shaped his incredible rise to prominence. We reveal the tale of Chew's impact on the tech industry through in-depth research and first-hand recollections, showing how he helped companies grow into industry titans, fueled the digital revolution, and opened the door for later breakthroughs.

"Shou Zi Chew: Architect of the New Tech Era" offers a perceptive glimpse into the thoughts of a visionary who is still influencing technological advancements. Along with providing readers with a portrait of a significant person, it also teaches them insightful lessons about resilience, creativity, and leadership amid a rapidly changing digital environment.

# CHAPTER 1: WHO IS SHOU ZI CHEW

Singaporean business executive and entrepreneur Shou Zi Chew is well-known for his important contributions to the technology sector. He is currently the CEO of ByteDance's well-known social media app TikTok, as of my most recent update.

Chew was the CFO and President of Xiaomi, a significant Chinese electronics and smartphone firm, before joining TikTok. His contributions to the expansion and advancement of these significant-tech enterprises have distinguished his career. Chew has a solid background in technology and finance, having worked for startups and investment firms before taking on senior positions.

Shou Zi Chew: Architect of the New Tech Era

# Childhood

On January 1, 1982, Shou Zi Chew was born in Singapore. He was exposed to a dynamic atmosphere that supported both traditional values and innovation while growing up in an energetic, multicultural city-state. Singapore's focus on technology and education created an environment that would have a big impact on his future professional path.

Chew grew up in a home where hard work and knowledge were valued. Since both of his parents were teachers, he was raised with academic achievement as a top priority. Chew showed early signs of a strong talent for learning and a deep interest in science and mathematics. His parents supported these hobbies by giving him the means and chance to pursue a variety of intellectual interests.

Chew thrived academically at elite local schools during his early years of education. He was accepted into Raffles Institution, one of Singapore's best secondary schools, as a result of his excellent academic achievement. He improved his scholastic abilities here, especially in areas like economics and mathematics, which would eventually be crucial to his profession.

Chew's participation in extracurricular activities complemented his early exposure to a demanding educational setting. His involvement in several school organizations and societies aided in the development of his organizational and leadership abilities.

In addition to being a vehicle for his personal development, these pursuits gave him early exposure to the dynamics of management and cooperation. In addition to his accomplishments in school and extracurricular activities, Chew's early years were characterized by an interest in technology and business. His objectives were probably motivated by Singapore's emphasis on innovation and its developing tech ecosystem.

Shou Zi Chew: Architect of the New Tech Era

He frequently participated in conversations regarding tech trends and their ramifications since he was captivated by the swift progress in technology. The distinct cultural and economic milieu of Singapore also influenced Chew's early years. Because of its emphasis on meritocracy and status as a major financial center, the city-state fostered an environment that was ideal for producing future leaders.

He developed a desire and a will to achieve in a cutthroat world as a result of this atmosphere. Chew maintained his academic excellence as he moved from secondary school to a university. He was able to get admission to the National University of Singapore (NUS) and began studying economics there. His academic success and involvement in campus events during his time at NUS set the groundwork for his future careers in technology and finance.

Early in life, Shou Zi Chew was drawn to a combination of demanding coursework, involvement in extracurricular activities, and a keen interest in technology. These encounters gave him a strong basis for his subsequent professional endeavors and gave him the information, motivation, and abilities that would help him advance into prominent roles in the international IT sector.

## Academics

Shou Zi Chew's academic trajectory is indicative of his dedication to excellence and his deep interest in the theoretical and applied facets of technology and business. His international schooling, which started in Singapore, was a major factor in forming his career and making him a well-known person in the computer sector.

Raffles Institution, one of Singapore's most prestigious secondary institutions, is where Chew started his academic career. Raffles Institution, which is renowned for its demanding academic standards and emphasis on fostering intellectual curiosity, gave Chew a strong

# Shou Zi Chew: Architect of the New Tech Era

foundation in topics that would be crucial to his success in the future.

Chew excelled in math and economics throughout his stay there, showing a strong grasp of subjects that both fascinated him and matched his developing interests in technology and finance.

After graduating from high school, Chew went on to study at the National University of Singapore (NUS), a prestigious university known for its demanding coursework. Chew studied for a Bachelor of Accountancy at NUS. His deliberate decision to pursue this area of study was motivated by a strong desire to comprehend the intricacies of economic and financial systems.

Chew was a standout student throughout his undergraduate career, receiving praise for his grasp of financial concepts and strong grades. Chew participated actively in several recreational and academic activities while attending NUS. He took part in conversations that

Shou Zi Chew: Architect of the New Tech Era

connected academic knowledge to real-world applications and spearheaded student-driven projects. His involvement improved his leadership and organizational abilities in addition to enriching his educational experience. He was placed on the Dean's List as a result of his academic excellence, which attests to his exceptional accomplishments and commitment to his studies.

Chew's desire to continue his education overseas reflects his commitment to academic success. He enrolled in the Master of Business Administration (MBA) program at University College London (UCL), one of the top colleges in the world. The institution's stellar reputation in business education and its global outlook on leadership and management were the main factors in his decision to attend UCL. Chew studied advanced business strategy, finance, and management courses at UCL.

His rigorous approach to comprehending complex business environments and formulating strategic solutions was a defining characteristic of his studies.

Shou Zi Chew: Architect of the New Tech Era

Chew participated in a variety of projects and case studies during his MBA program, which allowed him to apply theoretical knowledge to actual business challenges.

His stellar academic record at UCL and his distinguished graduation further cemented his reputation as an accomplished and well-informed business professional. His MBA program's knowledge and abilities had a significant influence on how he approached innovation and business leadership. Chew excelled academically outside of his official schooling. He has valued and taken advantage of educational opportunities throughout his career, whether they come from industry-related learning or professional development programs.

Because of his strong analytical framework and academic background, he has been able to make informed decisions and make a meaningful contribution to the organizations he has been a part of. In conclusion, Shou Zi Chew's remarkable performance at the

## Shou Zi Chew: Architect of the New Tech Era

secondary and tertiary levels is what distinguishes his academic accomplishments.

His educational background, which is distinguished by a combination of demanding coursework and real-world application, has been essential to his growth as a business and technology sector leader and innovator. His successful career has been fueled by his dedication to academic excellence and lifelong learning.

# CHAPTER 2: PROFESSIONAL JOURNEY

When Shou Zi Chew joined HTC, a well-known Taiwanese electronics company known for its breakthroughs in the smartphone and mobile technology business, his early career started to take form. His hiring by HTC signaled the start of a noteworthy phase of growth and success in his career.

Chew played a crucial part at HTC, which set the stage for his success in the IT sector going forward. Chew began his HTC career concentrating on strategic planning and financial management. He was responsible for overseeing financial operations, assessing market trends, and participating in the strategic efforts of the business.

# Shou Zi Chew: Architect of the New Tech Era

Chew spent this time improving HTC's financial models and procedures to maximize productivity and spur expansion. His services were crucial in helping HTC keep its competitive advantage in the quickly changing electronics industry.

Chew's early HTC career was noteworthy in part because of his engagement in product development. He was a major influence on how the business integrated new technologies into its product lines. HTC was able to better match its product offerings with the expectations of its customers because of Chew's insights into market demands and technological improvements. Given that HTC was negotiating a fiercely competitive market with new competitors and evolving consumer tastes, this alignment was especially crucial.

Chew's work on HTC's growth strategy and market positioning demonstrated his strategic ability. His contribution to the analysis of competitive environments and the identification of growth prospects was invaluable. Among his strategic goals were expanding

Shou Zi Chew: Architect of the New Tech Era

into untapped markets and strengthening HTC's position in the market by streamlining its product line.

During his tenure, Chew's ability to predict customer behavior and market trends was crucial in determining HTC's strategic path. While at HTC, Chew encountered various obstacles, such as fierce rivalry from competing firms and the requirement to quickly adjust to emerging technologies. He put new operational and financial techniques into place to deal with these issues. His ability to solve problems and think strategically enabled HTC to weather turbulent times and hold its position as the industry leader.

At HTC, Chew led with a collaborative approach and an emphasis on team building. To promote product innovation and guarantee successful market launches, he collaborated closely with cross-functional teams from engineering, marketing, and sales. HTC achieved its objectives in large part because of its ability to create a collaborative environment and cultivate strong relationships with team members.

## Shou Zi Chew: Architect of the New Tech Era

In his time at HTC, Chew accomplished several noteworthy firsts. He contributed to the triumphant introduction of multiple well-known devices that enabled HTC to establish itself as a top producer of smartphones. Strong financial performance and long-term growth were also made possible by his contributions to strategic planning and financial management.

Chew achieved several notable things throughout his early HTC career that paved the way for his future aspirations. His work at HTC showed off his proficiency in strategic planning and financial management as well as his capacity to influence product development and market positioning.

His later responsibilities and triumphs in the tech business were greatly influenced by the abilities and experiences he acquired during this time.

Shou Zi Chew made major contributions to product development, financial management, strategic planning, and market positioning during his early HTC career. His successes during this period made him a well-known personality in the technology industry and provided a solid basis for his future career.

## Position at Xiaomi

Shou Zi Chew joined Xiaomi, a leader in consumer electronics and technology globally, at a pivotal point in the company's development. Xiaomi, a company well-known for its creative thinking and assertive marketing tactics, offered Chew a special chance as well as several difficulties.

He had a broad range of duties at Xiaomi, including operational supervision, financial management, and strategic direction. Chew's career took a major turn after joining Xiaomi. He started as the Chief Financial Officer (CFO), in charge of managing the business's finances

## Shou Zi Chew: Architect of the New Tech Era

and spearheading its plan for international expansion. Managing Xiaomi's financial planning, reporting, and investor interactions were among his duties.

Chew was tasked with ensuring Xiaomi's explosive expansion was both sustainable and in line with the company's long-term strategic objectives. Simplifying Xiaomi's financial processes and boosting its financial transparency was one of his main goals. His main goal was to maximize the company's financial structure so that it could fund its ambitious ambitions for growth, which included expanding into new international markets and increasing the range of products it offered.

Chew's financial acumen was essential to preserving investor trust and fostering Xiaomi's ongoing expansion. Xiaomi observed a major improvement in its financial management procedures under Chew's direction. He put into practice a variety of financial techniques meant to strike a balance between profitability and expansion. This involved improving capital allocation,

## Shou Zi Chew: Architect of the New Tech Era

strengthening cost control, and streamlining the organization's budgeting procedures.

Chew's strategy for financial innovation entailed using data analytics and cutting-edge financial technologies to inform choices and boost productivity. In addition, Chew was crucial in overseeing Xiaomi's financial results as it went from being a privately held business to a publicly listed one. He played a key role in coordinating the financial parts of the listing process and guaranteeing regulatory compliance in the run-up to Xiaomi's 2018 initial public offering (IPO). For Xiaomi, the IPO was a huge turning point since it raised a substantial amount of money to support its growth and development initiatives.

Chew was involved in more than just finance management throughout Xiaomi's rapid global expansion; he also handled market positioning and strategic planning. In addition to studying competitive environments and creating strategies to break into new markets, he was involved in discovering and assessing new market prospects. Chew's proficiency in market

## Shou Zi Chew: Architect of the New Tech Era

analysis and strategic planning played a pivotal role in steering Xiaomi's global expansion and solidifying its foothold in a range of regions.

Chew's contributions were especially noteworthy during Xiaomi's attempts to enter Western markets, where the business encountered fierce competition from well-established competitors. His task involved modifying Xiaomi's product line and marketing approaches to conform to local customs and laws.

In addition to overseeing cross-border financial operations, he made sure Xiaomi's foreign endeavors were financially feasible as part of his global expansion responsibilities.

Chew had a significant impact on Xiaomi's technology and product innovation initiatives. He worked closely with the product development and engineering teams at Xiaomi to promote innovation and make sure the business stayed at the forefront of technical breakthroughs. Chew was involved in product strategy in

Shou Zi Chew: Architect of the New Tech Era

several ways, including analyzing emerging technologies, projecting how they could affect Xiaomi's product portfolio, and coordinating product development with industry developments.

He was also instrumental in helping Xiaomi develop an innovative culture. He was in favor of programs that promoted experimentation and creativity, which were essential components of Xiaomi's methodology for developing new products. His vision in this field helped Xiaomi establish a reputation as a leader in technology and enabled the company to provide customers with state-of-the-art goods.

Apart from his financial and strategic duties, Chew was also accountable for organizational growth and operational supervision. His focus was on enhancing the effectiveness of Xiaomi's worldwide operations, encompassing supply chain management, production procedures, and transportation.

## Shou Zi Chew: Architect of the New Tech Era

Chew's efforts in this field were directed toward improving Xiaomi's capacity to grow and satisfy the increasing demand for its goods. Chew worked on hiring and managing personnel as part of his organizational development responsibilities. He contributed to the development of a high-achieving team and made sure Xiaomi had the personnel and organizational framework necessary to support its expansion goals.

His leadership in this field was essential to keeping a vibrant and adaptable workforce that could spur innovation and accomplish organizational goals.

Chew faced many noteworthy obstacles and made tremendous progress throughout his time at Xiaomi. He managed the challenges of overseeing a quickly expanding international company while striking a balance between the requirement for strategic investments and the demands of financial success.

His leadership of Xiaomi during times of fast development and market turbulence was crucial to

Shou Zi Chew: Architect of the New Tech Era

maintaining the company's upward trajectory. Among Chew's noteworthy accomplishments was his part in Xiaomi's triumphant initial public offering (IPO), a significant occasion for the business.

Xiaomi was able to accelerate its expansion and diversify its product line thanks to the funds raised through the IPO. Many people agreed that Chew's leadership during this process was crucial to its success.

The growth and global positioning of Xiaomi were significantly influenced by Shou Zi Chew's involvement in the company. His contributions to strategic planning, operational control, and financial management were essential to Xiaomi's continuous growth. Xiaomi was able to drive innovation, overcome the obstacles of rapid expansion, and increase its market share globally because of Chew's leadership. In conclusion, Shou Zi Chew's position at Xiaomi was distinguished by a combination of operational savvy, strategic vision, and financial expertise.

Shou Zi Chew: Architect of the New Tech Era

His efforts had a significant impact on Xiaomi's course throughout a pivotal era of growth and development. Chew's impact at Xiaomi is a testament to his capacity to lead the company in technology globally, manage complexity, and spur growth.

## Significant breakthroughs and accomplishments

At Xiaomi, one of Shou Zi Chew's greatest accomplishments was the successful application of innovative finance techniques that guaranteed both continuous growth and operational excellence. Chew changed Xiaomi's financial management procedures as soon as he joined the business in his capacity as Chief Financial Officer (CFO).

Shou Zi Chew: Architect of the New Tech Era

His strategy involved incorporating data analytics and cutting-edge financial technologies into Xiaomi's financial processes, which significantly improved the business's efficiency and transparency.

One of Chew's financial management achievements was the creation of an advanced financial forecasting system that made use of real-time data to anticipate consumer and market trends. Xiaomi was able to allocate resources, invest, and budget more wisely because of this system. Xiaomi was able to increase profitability and save a lot of money by streamlining its cost management procedures under his direction.

His emphasis on capital allocation optimization allowed the business to make strategic investments in important areas like product development and market expansion.

An important accomplishment during Chew's time at Xiaomi was the business's triumphant 2018 initial public offering (IPO). Chew was essential to the successful completion of this highly anticipated initial public

## Shou Zi Chew: Architect of the New Tech Era

offering (IPO) in the technology sector. His duties included managing investor relations, supervising the financial parts of the listing process, and ensuring Xiaomi was ready for the public market by adhering to regulatory criteria.

Chew approached the IPO strategically, putting a lot of thought and preparation before it. He tried to present Xiaomi as a solid investment option by emphasizing its cutting-edge goods, steady financial results, and room for expansion.

The initial public offering (IPO) was a huge success, bringing in a significant amount of money to support Xiaomi's growth and development. It was a major turning point in Xiaomi's history, allowing the business to expand internationally and make investments in new industries and technology.

Xiaomi advanced its international expansion efforts significantly under Chew's financial direction. His ability to see trends in the market helped him spot and seize

## Shou Zi Chew: Architect of the New Tech Era

new chances. To guarantee a successful market entry and growth, Chew's approach to foreign expansion comprised thorough market study, competitive assessments, and strategic planning.

Chew was instrumental in Xiaomi's foray into several well-known areas, such as Western Europe and India. Among his endeavors was to modify Xiaomi's product lineup to accommodate local tastes and legal needs. For example, in India, Chew's team adapted Xiaomi's product line to suit local tastes by launching reasonably priced smartphones and cutting-edge technologies that appealed to the Indian consumer base. Xiaomi became a dominant force in the Indian smartphone market thanks to this localized strategy, which also helped the business boost its market share quickly.

Beyond his contributions to financial management, Chew made a major impact on product creation and technological advancements. His cooperation with the product development and engineering teams at Xiaomi was essential to the company's technological progress.

## Shou Zi Chew: Architect of the New Tech Era

Supporting projects that advanced technology and gave consumers access to cutting-edge goods was part of Chew's job description.

The creation of Xiaomi's Mi MIX series, which included ground-breaking features including bezel-less displays and sophisticated camera systems, was one of the noteworthy innovations during Chew's tenure. Chew's participation in these projects' financial assistance and strategic planning made it possible for Xiaomi to be at the forefront of technological advancement.

In addition to receiving praise for its technology and design, the Mi MIX series also raised the bar for smartphones. Chew's initiatives also helped Xiaomi expand into new product categories, like wearables and smart home appliances. Xiaomi has demonstrated its dedication to integrating technology into daily life and delivering a seamless user experience across several device categories through the launch of devices like the Mi Band and Mi Home ecosystem.

## Shou Zi Chew: Architect of the New Tech Era

Chew was also responsible for major supply chain optimization and operational improvements at Xiaomi. He improved production operations and streamlined Xiaomi's supply chain procedures as part of his focus on increasing operational efficiency. Chew's strategy for supply chain management focused on using technology and data analytics to improve manufacturing capacities, lower lead times, and optimize inventory levels.

The introduction of a just-in-time (JIT) inventory system, which minimized excess inventory and decreased storage costs, was one of the major accomplishments in this field. Xiaomi was able to maintain a lean and effective supply chain and react to changes in market demand more quickly because of this technology. Chew's work in this area helped Xiaomi expand its business and satisfy the rising demand for its goods throughout the world.

Enhancing Xiaomi's investor relations and financial communication techniques was another one of Chew's accomplishments. He worked to increase transparency

## Shou Zi Chew: Architect of the New Tech Era

and forge close bonds with analysts and investors in this regard. Chew's emphasis on efficient and transparent communication contributed to Xiaomi's standing as a stable and progressive business.

Chew started providing thorough financial reports, frequent investor updates, and in-depth briefings that shed light on Xiaomi's operations and long-term goals. These activities bolstered investor trust and provided support for the company's growth plans. To preserve goodwill with the investment community and make sure that Xiaomi's financial performance was appropriately reported and comprehended, Chew's efforts in this field were essential.

During Shou Zi Chew's time at Xiaomi, the firm saw several noteworthy inventions and accomplishments that had a big impact on its expansion and success. His influence was felt in the areas of financial management, international growth, technological innovation, and effective operations. Xiaomi's trajectory was shaped by Chew's strategic vision and leadership, which also

Shou Zi Chew: Architect of the New Tech Era

helped to secure Xiaomi's place as a top global technology company and fueled its ongoing evolution in the cutthroat tech industry.

## Chapter 3: Leadership at Xiaomi

The hiring of Shou Zi Chew as Xiaomi's CEO in April 2021 marked a turning point in the development of the business. With this shift, Xiaomi entered a new phase that included a leadership change and a strategic realignment. Chew's vast expertise and profound comprehension of Xiaomi's operations and strategic goals made him an ideal candidate to manage the firm.

He had previously held the positions of President of International Business and Chief Financial Officer (CFO). The announcement of the appointment coincided with Xiaomi's efforts to navigate a world market that was changing quickly, marked by growing tech industry competition and shifting customer tastes.

His elevation to the position of CEO was viewed as a calculated decision to make use of his financial savvy,

## Shou Zi Chew: Architect of the New Tech Era

global experience, and leadership abilities to guide Xiaomi through these difficulties and seize fresh chances.

Following his appointment as CEO, Chew presented a strategic plan designed to strengthen Xiaomi's position in the market and promote long-term growth. His style of leadership was centered on various important areas. Chew stressed the significance of bolstering Xiaomi's technological and product innovation core strengths. His goal was to uphold Xiaomi's reputation for producing innovative, high-quality goods while keeping the business at the forefront of technological development. This involved concentrating on the creation of wearable technology, smart home appliances, and new cell phones.

Part of Chew's plan was quickening Xiaomi's efforts to expand internationally. He aimed to expand Xiaomi's market share in strategic areas and break into new countries to capitalize on the company's prior foreign accomplishments. Chew's background in overseeing

Shou Zi Chew: Architect of the New Tech Era

Xiaomi's global operations was essential in developing and implementing plans for market entry and expansion.

Improving operational efficiency throughout Xiaomi's international operations was one of Chew's top priorities. This entailed streamlining the supply chain, cutting expenses, and enhancing the production procedures to facilitate the company's expansion goals. Chew's experience in operations and finance management gave him a solid platform on which to push these advancements.

Chew understood that research and development (R&D) was essential to preserving Xiaomi's competitive advantage. To achieve and create new technologies that may set Xiaomi's products apart from the competition, he sought to enhance R&D spending. Under Chew's direction, efforts to promote technological advancement and creativity were supported, along with an innovative culture.

Shou Zi Chew: Architect of the New Tech Era

Chew also placed a high priority on improving customer assistance, user interfaces, and product quality. His mission was to make sure Xiaomi's goods and services fulfilled strict quality requirements and provide value for customers.

Xiaomi launched several significant programs and activities under Chew's direction that were in line with his strategic vision: Promoting product innovation was one of Chew's main priorities. Xiaomi launched several new product lines during his leadership, including sophisticated smartphones with cutting-edge technologies like improved camera systems, 5G connection, and AI capabilities.

In keeping with Chew's goal of incorporating technology into as many facets of everyday life as possible, the firm also increased the range of wearables and smart home appliances in its ecosystem. Chew focused its global business strategy on developing and developing markets. Xiaomi kept expanding its footprint in Europe, Southeast Asia, and India. Chew's leadership included creating

## Shou Zi Chew: Architect of the New Tech Era

strategic alliances to increase market penetration and modifying product offers to satisfy local preferences and legal needs.

Chew gave corporate responsibility and sustainability a lot of weight. Xiaomi made steps to lessen its environmental impact, such as encouraging recycling programs and enhancing manufacturing processes' energy efficiency. Xiaomi's leadership, led by Chew, sought to establish the company as a socially and environmentally conscious corporate citizen.

Chew promoted Xiaomi's digital transformation by utilizing technology to improve consumer relations and company procedures. To better understand customer demands and encourage participation, this involved putting advanced data analytics, AI-driven insights, and digital marketing techniques into practice.

There were difficulties throughout Chew's time as CEO. In addition to dealing with trade barriers and geopolitical issues that affected its international operations, Xiaomi

## Shou Zi Chew: Architect of the New Tech Era

had to contend with fierce competition from other IT behemoths.

Chew used proactive problem-solving and strategic agility to overcome these obstacles. Trade limitations and geopolitical conflicts posed challenges for Xiaomi, especially in regions like the US. Chew's strategy entailed investigating alternative markets and diversifying supply chains to lessen the impact of these problems on Xiaomi's commercial operations.

Numerous technology firms experienced supply chain disruptions as a result of the COVID-19 pandemic and other worldwide events. Chew's emphasis on streamlining the supply chain and enhancing operational effectiveness enabled Xiaomi to overcome these obstacles and keep its capacity for production and delivery.

Chew highlighted the significance of ongoing innovation and technical improvement to stay ahead in a competitive market. Xiaomi's dedication to producing

Shou Zi Chew: Architect of the New Tech Era

high-quality products and its investment in research and development were crucial tactics for preserving its competitive advantage.

The general public and industry analysts reacted favorably to Chew's selection as CEO. His past accomplishments and experience at Xiaomi added to his self-assurance as a leader. Chew was acknowledged by analysts and industry experts as a strategic thinker with a strong background in technology and a proven track record of effective management.

Chew's emphasis on innovation, worldwide expansion, and operational efficiency was well-received. Transparency, strategic vision, and a dedication to driving growth were hallmarks of his leadership style. Strong and favorable opinions of his leadership were a result of his attempts to strengthen Xiaomi's position in the market and solve issues facing the industry.

An important turning point for Xiaomi was the appointment of Shou Zi Chew as CEO. His experience,

Shou Zi Chew: Architect of the New Tech Era

leadership skills, and strategic vision were crucial in helping Xiaomi navigate through a time of explosive development and transition. Chew's emphasis on innovation, international growth, operational excellence, and corporate social responsibility influenced Xiaomi's course and set up the business for long-term success in the cutthroat technology sector.

During his time as CEO, he led Xiaomi with vision and propelled the company's development while bolstering its international footprint.

## Strategic objectives and vision

As the CEO of Xiaomi, Shou Zi Chew's strategic vision was built around several fundamental principles that sought to strengthen the business's standing as a leader in innovation and technology worldwide. His strategy was all-encompassing, including a wide range of corporate

## Shou Zi Chew: Architect of the New Tech Era

operations, market positioning, and potential growth areas for Xiaomi.

Enhancing Xiaomi's technology leadership, promoting international expansion, and maximizing operational efficiency were the cornerstones of Chew's strategy.

Reiterating Xiaomi's position as a leader in technology was a key component of Chew's strategic plan. He underlined how crucial R&D and innovation are to keeping a competitive edge and satisfying changing customer demands. Under his direction, Xiaomi made significant investments in state-of-the-art R&D to push the boundaries of technology. This included investigating cutting-edge display technologies, 5G connectivity, and artificial intelligence (AI) as new technical horizons.

Chew's plan entailed establishing an innovative culture at Xiaomi and promoting cross-functional cooperation and original problem-solving. The goal of this strategy was to hasten the creation of innovative goods and technology. Expansion of Xiaomi's R&D facilities and

## Shou Zi Chew: Architect of the New Tech Era

collaborations with top technical research institutes were important efforts. Chew wanted to create an exceptional user experience and establish new benchmarks for the industry by spearheading the development of fundamental technologies and incorporating them into Xiaomi's product line.

Another essential component of Chew's strategy plan was his goal for worldwide expansion. Seeing the value of global markets for Xiaomi's expansion, Chew concentrated on growing the company's footprint in both developed and emerging nations. His strategy combined regional customization, market penetration, and strategic alliances.

Chew planned to take advantage of Xiaomi's competitive pricing and value-for-money promise in emerging areas, such as India and Southeast Asia. To increase market reach, he set out to create effective distribution networks and solid local alliances. Chew concentrated on establishing Xiaomi as a premium brand in developed areas, like as Europe and North America, by introducing

## Shou Zi Chew: Architect of the New Tech Era

high-end goods and premium features. This two-pronged strategy was intended to seize a wide range of market prospects and propel worldwide income expansion.

As part of Chew's worldwide expansion strategy, Xiaomi's goods and services were modified to satisfy local standards and tastes. This includes regional standards compliance, tailored marketing efforts, and locally relevant product offerings. Xiaomi's strategy was customized for each area to improve customer happiness and solidify the company's position in the global market.

Chew's strategy vision placed a strong emphasis on operational efficiency, to streamline Xiaomi's business procedures to meet its expansion goals. Chew understood that sustaining operational excellence was crucial to growing the business's activities and guaranteeing its long-term viability. Chew implemented modern logistics solutions, improved production processes, and streamlined supply chain management as part of its operational efficiency strategy.

## Shou Zi Chew: Architect of the New Tech Era

He underlined the significance of having a flexible supply chain that could adjust to shifts in consumer demand and interruptions in the supply chain. To improve responsiveness and cost-effectiveness, this entailed lowering lead times, raising manufacturing capacities, and optimizing inventory levels.

Chew also concentrated on using automation and data analytics to create operational gains. To increase productivity, cut expenses, and boost overall performance, Xiaomi employed cutting-edge technologies to assess and optimize company processes. To support Xiaomi's aggressive expansion objectives and make sure the business could meet the expectations of a dynamic global market, Chew's dedication to operational excellence was essential.

Ensuring that Xiaomi's products and services provided outstanding value and improving the customer experience was central to Chew's strategic goal. Chew understood that fostering long-term success and fostering brand loyalty required a customer-centric strategy.

Shou Zi Chew: Architect of the New Tech Era

Chew's approach comprised a thorough analysis of the requirements and preferences of the consumer. This involved spending money on user research, examining market trends, and obtaining input to guide the creation and enhancement of new products. Chew sought to build emotionally engaging user experiences for Xiaomi's products by fusing customer data into their design and functionality.

Chew's goal encompassed not only new product innovation but also enhanced customer support and service. This required improving Xiaomi's after-sales service, offering prompt assistance, and skillfully handling client complaints.

He showed His dedication to customer satisfaction through many initiatives, including the expansion of its service centers, enhancement of response times, and provision of extensive warranty and repair services.

## Shou Zi Chew: Architect of the New Tech Era

Chew had a strong commitment to corporate responsibility and sustainability as part of its strategic objective. Acknowledging the growing significance of social and environmental issues, Chew sought to establish Xiaomi as a socially and environmentally conscious corporate citizen.

One of Chew's sustainability strategies was to take steps to lessen Xiaomi's environmental effects. This included reducing waste, boosting recycling initiatives, and enhancing the energy efficiency of production processes. Under Chew's direction, Xiaomi's operations were streamlined to include eco-friendly procedures and high sustainability targets.

Furthermore, Chew highlighted the importance of corporate social responsibility (CSR) in Xiaomi's approach. This included funding educational initiatives, encouraging diversity and inclusion within the workforce, and supporting community development projects. Chew sought to improve Xiaomi's standing with stakeholders and fortify ties with them by

## Shou Zi Chew: Architect of the New Tech Era

coordinating the company's business operations with social and environmental principles.

Chew's strategic strategy for the future included laying the groundwork for expansion and innovation. His strategy consisted of locating new trends and technological advancements that would propel Xiaomi into its next stage of growth. This involved looking into potential in fields including improved health technologies, networked devices, and smart cities.

To maintain Xiaomi's standing as a top technology firm, Chew also saw that the company should continue to grow through strategic alliances, acquisitions, and joint ventures. To remain ahead of technology improvements and broaden its market reach, Xiaomi formed connections with other industry heavyweights and invested in potential startups.

As Xiaomi's CEO, Shou Zi Chew formulated a comprehensive and forward-looking strategic plan to propel the company's expansion and prosperity. His

Shou Zi Chew: Architect of the New Tech Era

emphasis on operational effectiveness, customer experience, sustainability, technological leadership, global expansion, and future innovation put Xiaomi in a position to successfully negotiate the challenges of the global tech scene and seize new opportunities. Xiaomi's trajectory and sustained leadership in the technology sector were greatly influenced by Chew's strategic goals and activities.

## Important programs and projects

Shou Zi Chew's commitment to driving Xiaomi's product innovation forward was a pillar of his leadership. Understanding that technological leadership and distinctiveness are essential for gaining a competitive edge, Chew gave top priority to several important projects that will advance technology and improve Xiaomi's product line.

Shou Zi Chew: Architect of the New Tech Era

Xiaomi made large investments in research and development (R&D) to support technological advancements under Chew's leadership. To speed up the creation of cutting-edge technologies, this included Xiaomi's R&D centers are being expanded throughout the world.

A noteworthy breakthrough was the improvement of the Mi MIX line, which included breakthroughs like bezel-less screens and under-display camera technology. These developments not only raised the bar for smartphone design but also showed Xiaomi's dedication to producing products with the best possible functionality and aesthetics.

Chew also concentrated on incorporating machine learning and artificial intelligence (AI) into Xiaomi's product line. Among the initiatives was the creation of AI-powered smartphone features like customized user interfaces and sophisticated camera capabilities. AI improvements were added to Xiaomi's MIUI interface to increase user experience and device performance. To

## Shou Zi Chew: Architect of the New Tech Era

establish a unified and intelligent environment, Chew also promoted the extension of AI applications into other product categories, such as wearables and smart home appliances.

An aggressive plan for worldwide expansion was part of Chew's plan to increase Xiaomi's market share in important foreign markets. His strategy was multifaceted, emphasizing strategic alliances, market penetration, and regional adaption. Chew oversaw several important initiatives, one of which was Xiaomi's increased entry into the Western market. To satisfy the high standards and discerning tastes of customers in places like North America and Europe, flagship items and premium offerings have to be introduced.

Xiaomi prioritized quality, innovation, and value to become a competitive competitor in these markets. Chew's approach consisted of taking advantage of Xiaomi's compelling value offer in developing areas like Southeast Asia and India to gain market share. This includes introducing smartphones that are both

## Shou Zi Chew: Architect of the New Tech Era

reasonably priced and highly functional, as well as forming reliable local alliances to improve distribution and consumer interaction.

Localized software and features were among the activities that Chew oversaw to adjust Xiaomi's goods and services to suit local needs and tastes.

The key to scaling Xiaomi's operations and achieving its growth goals was Chew's strategic focus on operational efficiency. To improve operating procedures and optimize Xiaomi's supply chain, several significant projects were implemented. The installation of a complex supply chain management system, which aims to maximize inventory levels, shorten lead times, and enhance overall logistics effectiveness, was one significant project. With the help of this technology, which combined automation and sophisticated data analytics to improve supply chain visibility, Xiaomi was able to more quickly adapt to market demands and minimize supply chain interruptions.

## Shou Zi Chew: Architect of the New Tech Era

Chew spearheaded initiatives to improve production procedures through the acquisition of intelligent manufacturing technologies. Using automation and robotics on production lines to boost productivity and consistency was one aspect of this. Xiaomi sought to increase production capacity while upholding high standards of quality by incorporating these technologies.

Customer experience improvement rose to the top of the priority list under Chew's direction. To improve Xiaomi's service offerings and guarantee that clients receive outstanding support, some significant initiatives were introduced. An important undertaking was growing Xiaomi's network of customer support representatives. As part of this, more service centers were opened throughout the world, especially in areas where the number of clients was rising.

Chew's approach was centered on expediting repair and support turnaround times and enhancing service accessibility. Additionally, Xiaomi unveiled improved online help tools, such as chatbots and AI-powered support, to deliver prompt and efficient customer service. Creating extensive warranty and service plans aimed at fostering client happiness and trust was another of Chew's goals.

To meet the diverse needs of our customers, this entailed providing flexible service alternatives and extending warranty periods. Chew gave corporate responsibility and sustainability a lot of weight in Xiaomi's business operations. To solve social and environmental challenges, several significant initiatives were launched.

The introduction of environmentally friendly approaches into Xiaomi's production processes was one significant effort. This included making steps to cut waste, increase energy efficiency, and lower carbon emissions. Setting high standards for sustainability and making investments in tools and procedures to help achieve them were key components of Chew's approach.

Additionally, Chew spearheaded efforts to advance corporate social responsibility (CSR) within the

## Shou Zi Chew: Architect of the New Tech Era

business. This includes funding educational initiatives, encouraging diversity and inclusivity within Xiaomi, and supporting community development projects. With these efforts, Xiaomi hopes to strengthen its good social effect and establish itself as a reputable corporate citizen.

A crucial element of Chew's strategic plan was growing Xiaomi's product ecosystem. Creating a unified and smooth experience for users across different device categories was the aim. The creation of the Mi Home ecosystem, which combines Xiaomi's wearables, smart home appliances, and other linked goods, was one of the major projects. With the help of a single platform, users will be able to operate and interact with their devices in a more unified and intuitive manner thanks to this project.

Chew planned to improve device compatibility and broaden the ecosystem to encompass new product categories. Chew concentrated on fusing the Xiaomi environment with other online businesses and platforms. As part of this, Xiaomi partnered with outside

Shou Zi Chew: Architect of the New Tech Era

developers and service providers to improve the features and worth of its products.

Xiaomi sought to provide a comprehensive and user-friendly experience through the expansion of its ecosystem and the promotion of integration with external services.

Chew envisioned a digital transformation in which Xiaomi's business processes and consumer interaction would be improved through the use of technology.

Several significant projects were started to promote digital innovation. Using AI and sophisticated data analytics to enhance operational effectiveness and decision-making was one of the project's main goals. This involved enhancing product development, marketing strategy optimization, and consumer behavior insights through the use of data analytics. Chew planned to increase Xiaomi's skills in these areas by making investments in digital tools and technologies.

## Shou Zi Chew: Architect of the New Tech Era

Chew also oversaw initiatives to improve Xiaomi's e-commerce and digital marketing systems. This involved enhancing Xiaomi's online sales channels, creating customized consumer engagement tactics, and creating focused digital marketing campaigns. Xiaomi sought to expand its market, boost revenue, and improve the general customer experience by utilizing digital technology.

During Shou Zi Chew's stint as CEO, several significant projects and activities that were essential to Xiaomi's strategic vision were initiated and carried out. His emphasis on promoting product innovation, international growth, operational effectiveness, customer experience, sustainability, ecosystem development, and digital transformation contributed to Xiaomi's rise to prominence as a top technology business with a significant presence around the globe.

Xiaomi grew as a result of Chew's leadership in these domains, which also strengthened Xiaomi's dedication to technology

Shou Zi Chew: Architect of the New Tech Era

# CHAPTER 3:INFLUENCE ON XIAOMI'S GROWTH

Shou Zi Chew has had a significant and wide-ranging impact on Xiaomi's development, propelling the business to new heights in many areas. Xiaomi's trajectory has been greatly influenced by his leadership and strategic choices, which have affected the company's general corporate strategy, market presence, financial success, and product innovation.

Chew's effect on Xiaomi's growth may be examined from the perspectives of several important factors, including market expansion, corporate culture, product innovation, financial performance, and operational efficiency.

## Shou Zi Chew: Architect of the New Tech Era

During Chew's time at Xiaomi, the company's operational effectiveness and financial performance have significantly improved. His experience as a CFO gave him the know-how to improve Xiaomi's resource allocation and financial management plans. Chew made a significant contribution when he focused on using advanced data analytics and forecasting techniques to optimize financial operations.

Xiaomi was able to more accurately forecast market trends, control expenses, and distribute resources thanks to these techniques. Chew led efforts to optimize Xiaomi's cost control procedures, which increased profit margins and produced notable savings. He implemented strict budgeting procedures and improved financial controls as part of his efforts to improve the company's financial strategies.

Xiaomi was able to maintain both strong profitability and rapid development thanks to this financial discipline. Chew also improved operational efficiency by concentrating on production procedures and supply chain optimization.

To improve inventory control and logistics, he adopted data-driven solutions and cutting-edge technologies in his supply chain management strategy. Through process optimization, Xiaomi was able to lower costs, shorten lead times, and better adapt to shifts in consumer demand. The efficiency improvements resulting from these initiatives helped Xiaomi expand its business and satisfy the rising demand for its goods around the world.

Xiaomi's efforts to expand its global market gained considerable traction under Chew's direction. His strategic vision for global expansion had a pivotal role in steering the organization's foray into novel and varied markets. Chew's strategy combined regional adaptability, market intelligence, and strategic alliances.

Chew concentrated on establishing Xiaomi as a premium brand in well-established countries including North America and Europe. To satisfy the desires of customers

## Shou Zi Chew: Architect of the New Tech Era

in these areas, high-end items and premium features have to be introduced. Chew's approach encompassed establishing alliances with nearby distributors and retailers to augment market share and prominence.

Consequently, Xiaomi was able to grow its market share in these cutthroat areas and solidified its position as a major force in the global tech sector. Chew's approach took use of Xiaomi's value-for-money offering in developing areas like Southeast Asia and India. Xiaomi was able to quickly gain market share and establish a strong brand presence by providing high-quality products at an inexpensive price.

Chew's initiatives in these areas included bolstering regional distribution networks and localizing goods and services to suit local tastes. This strategy helped Xiaomi enter these important areas and also aided in its quick expansion and widespread uptake.

Under Chew's direction, product innovation has been the main driver of Xiaomi's expansion. His strategic vision

## Shou Zi Chew: Architect of the New Tech Era

placed a strong emphasis on the necessity of ongoing innovation and technological improvement to keep a competitive edge. Chew had a significant impact on Xiaomi's approach to product development, resulting in several important projects that strengthened the business's standing as a pioneer in technology.

To advance technical innovations and improve Xiaomi's product line, Chew promoted large expenditures in research and development (R&D). This included the creation of sophisticated smartphones with cutting-edge capabilities like under-display fingerprint sensors, 5G connection, and AI-driven cameras. Under Chew's direction, the Mi MIX series unveiled ground-breaking technology that raised the bar for smartphone functionality and design.

Chew's impact went beyond smartphones to encompass Xiaomi's wider range of products, such as wearables and smart home appliances. He created a smooth and linked user experience by strategically focusing on integrating technology across several product categories. Chew

## Shou Zi Chew: Architect of the New Tech Era

demonstrated its dedication to providing a logical and well-thought-out product range that improved user convenience and engagement by expanding the Mi Home ecosystem.

Xiaomi has grown significantly as a result of Chew's corporate culture approach and leadership style. His focus on encouraging a climate of creativity, openness, and cooperation helped to create a vibrant and progressive workplace. Chew's leadership style promoted innovative problem-solving and cross-functional cooperation, both of which were critical for fostering innovation and accomplishing strategic objectives.

Chew's emphasis on staff engagement and talent development was also a major contributor to Xiaomi's expansion. He placed a high priority on luring and keeping elite personnel by fostering an atmosphere that encouraged advancement in the workplace. This involved encouraging a culture of reward and

## Shou Zi Chew: Architect of the New Tech Era

recognition and giving staff members the chance to participate in high-impact projects.

Chew's leadership also included a resolute dedication to openness and moral business conduct. By encouraging a culture of honesty and responsibility, Chew strengthened Xiaomi's standing as a trustworthy business. This strategy bolstered Xiaomi's good brand image and long-term performance by fostering trust with stakeholders such as partners, investors, and consumers.

Xiaomi's growth and rise to prominence in the sector have been largely fueled by Chew's strategic positioning of the company in the technology market. His strategy consisted of seeing new trends and business possibilities and then using Xiaomi's advantages to take advantage of them.

A key component of Chew's strategy goal was differentiating Xiaomi via value and innovation. Xiaomi was able to establish itself as a leader in the industry by emphasizing technology development and providing

## Shou Zi Chew: Architect of the New Tech Era

premium goods at affordable costs. Xiaomi benefited from Chew's leadership in this field, which allowed it to draw in a large client base and successfully take on other tech behemoths.

Chew's impact was also felt in Xiaomi's strategy for technical integration and digital transformation. Xiaomi's operational efficiency and consumer engagement were improved by his emphasis on utilizing digital marketing methods, artificial intelligence, and data analytics. These initiatives helped Xiaomi stay ahead of the competition in the technology sector and adjust to shifting market conditions.

Chew's dedication to corporate social responsibility and sustainability has been a vital component of Xiaomi's expansion plan. His leadership in this field was a reflection of his understanding of how important social and environmental issues are becoming on the world stage. Xiaomi carried out some programs under Chew's leadership to lessen its impact on the environment and encourage corporate social responsibility.

## Shou Zi Chew: Architect of the New Tech Era

This includes initiatives to lower waste, promote recycling programs, and increase the energy efficiency of production operations.

In addition to establishing challenging objectives, Chew's emphasis on sustainability involves incorporating eco-friendly procedures into Xiaomi's daily operations. Chew's approach to corporate social responsibility included funding social and community development projects.

Xiaomi participated in several CSR endeavors, such as educational initiatives, community service projects, and campaigns to support diversity and inclusion. Through these initiatives, Xiaomi was able to strengthen its standing as a conscientious corporate citizen and reaffirm its dedication to generating positive social impact.

The long-term course of Xiaomi has been significantly shaped by Chew's strategic planning for expansion. His

## Shou Zi Chew: Architect of the New Tech Era

method comprised seeing new opportunities, establishing precise growth goals, and creating plans to reach these targets. To propel Xiaomi into its next stage of development, Chew's strategy for the company's expansion involved investigating new markets and technology. This required making investments in fields like linked gadgets, smart cities, and cutting-edge medical technologies.

Chew set up Xiaomi for long-term success and innovation by keeping ahead of technology trends and foreseeing consumer wants. Scalability and flexibility were also key considerations in Chew's strategic planning. Creating adaptable tactics that could address shifting market dynamics and new obstacles was part of his strategy. This made Xiaomi adaptable and strong in the face of a changing international landscape.

Shou Zi Chew has had a profound and revolutionary impact on Xiaomi's expansion. The company's financial performance, market expansion, product innovation, corporate culture, and strategic orientation have all been

Shou Zi Chew: Architect of the New Tech Era

profoundly impacted by his leadership. Xiaomi has become a dominant force in the global technology industry thanks to Chew's emphasis on corporate responsibility, worldwide market expansion, operational efficiency, and technological leadership.

In addition to shaping Xiaomi's current state, his strategic vision and activities have established the groundwork for the company's future expansion and development.

## Significant technological developments

Under Shou Zi Chew's leadership at Xiaomi has elevated the business to the forefront of the world's technology scene. His emphasis on innovation and cutting-edge technology had a significant impact on Xiaomi's technological strategy and product development. Xiaomi launched several significant technology projects under

## Shou Zi Chew: Architect of the New Tech Era

Chew's direction that have improved the company's competitive edge and established new benchmarks in the tech sector.

Under Chew's direction, Xiaomi made significant strides in technology, with a particular emphasis on smartphones. Chew promoted the creation of high-performing gadgets with cutting-edge features intended to boost smartphone technology. The launch of the Mi MIX series, which included cutting-edge innovations like bezel-less displays and creative camera solutions, is one such example.

Chew spearheaded efforts to create cutting-edge screen designs, and Xiaomi achieved notable advancements in this area. The Mi MIX series used under-display camera technologies and improved screen-to-body ratios to provide nearly bezel-less screens. OLED and AMOLED screen integration improved display quality even more, giving customers sharp colors and strong contrast ratios. In addition to enhancing visual experiences, this

Shou Zi Chew: Architect of the New Tech Era

emphasis on display innovation raised the bar for smartphone design.

Xiaomi prioritized the advancement of smartphone camera technology under Chew's direction. The company unveiled products with multi-lens camera systems that featured sophisticated computational photography features together with high-resolution sensors. Xiaomi's camera technology became known for its innovations, which included improved zoom capabilities, night mode photography, and AI-driven picture processing. Thanks to these developments, users can now take excellent photos and films, establishing Xiaomi as a pioneer in mobile photography.

Xiaomi integrated 5G capabilities into its smartphone lineup, making the rollout of 5G technology a major area of concentration. Under Chew's direction, 5G network-enabling equipment with increased connectivity, reduced latency, and quicker data rates were developed. A major advancement in mobile technology was made with the release of 5G-enabled smartphones, which

## Shou Zi Chew: Architect of the New Tech Era

allowed users to benefit from improved network speed and support for newly developed applications like augmented reality (AR) and virtual reality (VR).

One aspect of Chew's strategy plan was to broaden Xiaomi's product line beyond smartphones to include a variety of smart home appliances. The idea was to combine different electronic goods into one ecosystem, resulting in a unified and connected user experience. This idea was made possible in large part by Xiaomi's Mi Home platform, which offered a centralized interface for managing and controlling smart devices.

To improve the experience of owning a smart home, Xiaomi unveiled a range of connected devices. Smart appliances, lights, security cameras, and speakers were among them. The Mi Home app's connection with these gadgets made it easy for customers to automate and control their homes. Chew's pioneering work in this field sought to develop an all-encompassing smart home ecosystem that provided efficiency, ease, and improved user experiences.

Shou Zi Chew: Architect of the New Tech Era

Xiaomi's smart home approach heavily relied on automation and artificial intelligence (AI). Chew's idea was to employ AI to improve user experience and gadget functionality. For instance, Xiaomi's smart speakers now have AI-powered voice assistants built in, allowing customers to operate their smart home appliances using voice commands. To increase productivity and optimize daily operations, automation capabilities like scheduling and remote control were also added.

Under Chew's direction, Xiaomi made significant strides in wearable technology. The company increased the variety of wearables in its lineup by adding smartwatches and fitness trackers that are intended to give consumers complete activity and health tracking. For example, the Mi Band series gained popularity for its feature-rich and reasonably priced offers, which included activity tracking, sleep tracking, and heart rate monitoring.

## Shou Zi Chew: Architect of the New Tech Era

Xiaomi's wearables now include cutting-edge health monitoring features thanks to Chew's focus on health innovation. Sensors on the devices were used to monitor blood oxygen levels, stress levels, and heart rate variability, among other health measures. Xiaomi was positioned as a leader in the wearable technology market thanks to its emphasis on health and wellness, which was in line with consumers' growing interest in fitness and health management.

In addition to GPS tracking and sports modes, Xiaomi's wearables have integrated health app integration. Users were given comprehensive insights into their physical activities and general well-being because of these features. Chew's pioneering work in this field sought to provide consumers with a comprehensive health monitoring solution by fusing cutting-edge technology with useful features.

Using artificial intelligence (AI) and machine learning to improve Xiaomi's product offerings and company operations was part of Chew's strategic vision.

## Shou Zi Chew: Architect of the New Tech Era

Numerous product categories, such as wearables, smartphones, and smart home appliances, have incorporated AI technologies. Enhancing device functionality, user experiences, and performance were the goals of this integration.

Xiaomi has included several AI-driven features, like voice assistants, sophisticated image recognition, and personalized suggestions, into its products. Advanced capabilities like facial recognition, scene identification, and real-time photo upgrades are made possible by smartphones with AI-powered image processing. Voice assistants gave users information access and hands-free control when they were incorporated into smart gadgets. To assess user activity and offer tailored suggestions for apps, content, and services, machine learning algorithms were also used.

One of Chew's major initiatives was the creation of smart assistants. Xiao Ai, Xiaomi's AI assistant, was created to offer consumers a variety of features, including information retrieval, voice commands, and

## Shou Zi Chew: Architect of the New Tech Era

management over smart homes. By utilizing natural language processing and machine learning to increase the precision and effectiveness of voice-based instructions, Chew's focus on improving smart assistants sought to produce more intuitive and responsive user engagements.

Xiaomi's technological breakthroughs were made possible in large part by Chew's leadership in the fields of next-generation networking and the Internet of Things (IoT). The company concentrated on creating Internet of Things solutions that allowed different systems and devices to communicate with ease.

The advancement of IoT applications was greatly aided by the incorporation of 5G technology. Faster and more dependable communication between linked devices was made possible by Xiaomi's efforts to support 5G connection in its devices. As a result, IoT applications including real-time data processing, remote monitoring, and smart home automation performed better.

Shou Zi Chew: Architect of the New Tech Era

Xiaomi approached the Internet of Things by building a single ecosystem that made it possible for various devices to function as one. By introducing standards and protocols for device compatibility, the firm made it possible for consumers to integrate and manage several devices on a single platform. Chew's emphasis on cross-device interoperability was meant to improve user experience in general and make managing connected devices easier.

To keep ahead of the competition in the tech industry, Xiaomi actively investigated upcoming trends and technologies under Chew's direction. To find and seize new technological breakthroughs, the corporation made research and development investments.

Xiaomi's interest in these immersive experiences was demonstrated by the creation of goods and technology that integrated these technologies. To produce unique and captivating user experiences, the company investigated AR and VR applications in sectors like gaming, education, and entertainment.

## Shou Zi Chew: Architect of the New Tech Era

Additional areas of interest were the investigation of blockchain technology and developments in security. Xiaomi looked into the possible uses of blockchain in the areas of transparency, authentication, and data security. Chew placed a strong focus on security technologies to allay growing worries about privacy and data protection in the digital era.

Xiaomi made significant investments in research and development (R&D), demonstrating Chew's dedication to technical growth. The corporation set up research facilities in important technology hotspots across the globe, extending its global R&D network.

Advanced manufacturing techniques, materials science, semiconductor technology, and other cutting-edge fields were all included in Xiaomi's R&D endeavors. Chew's management encouraged the creation of novel ideas and proprietary technology that boosted the business's technological advantage.

Shou Zi Chew: Architect of the New Tech Era

Xiaomi's R&D approach also included partnerships and collaborations with top universities, research centers, and technological companies. These collaborations made access to cutting-edge technologies, cooperative research projects, and knowledge sharing possible. Chew's emphasis on strategic partnerships was meant to spur innovation and hasten the release of cutting-edge products.

Xiaomi's status as a top technology innovator has been greatly shaped by Shou Zi Chew's influence on the company's technological innovations. Under his direction, advancements in wearable technology, artificial intelligence, smart home integration, smartphone technology, and next-generation connectivity were greatly accelerated.

Xiaomi is now at the forefront of technological innovation thanks to Chew's strategic emphasis on R&D, emerging technologies, and cross-device integration, which has fueled the company's growth and success in a cutthroat international market. Chew has significantly

Shou Zi Chew: Architect of the New Tech Era

contributed to the advancement of Xiaomi's technological capabilities and the direction of the company through a combination of visionary leadership, wise investments, and a dedication to excellence.

## Strategy and Market Positioning

Xiaomi has implemented a complex market positioning and strategy approach under the direction of Shou Zi Chew, which has had a major impact on the company's standing internationally and growth trajectory. Chew's strategy was created to take into account several market dynamics, such as customer segmentation, competitive differentiation, brand positioning, and strategic alliances. His all-encompassing strategy sought to make Xiaomi a major force in the world technology market while accommodating local variances and new trends.

## Shou Zi Chew: Architect of the New Tech Era

Xiaomi's dedication to providing premium goods at affordable costs was the cornerstone of its market positioning strategy. Xiaomi's value for money was highlighted by Chew as a crucial differentiator in a crowded market. Xiaomi drew in cost-conscious customers who desired superior performance without breaking the bank by providing cutting-edge technology and unique features at reasonable costs.

Chew sought to improve Xiaomi's brand perception in the premium and lifestyle segments while upholding a strong value-for-money proposition. This entailed launching high-end goods with state-of-the-art features and technology, like flagship smartphones and the Mi MIX series. To cater to a wider spectrum of customers, including those in the luxury segment, Xiaomi aimed to offer products that blended cutting-edge technology with fashionable design.

Under Chew's direction, Xiaomi emphasized its focus on technology innovation in its market positioning approach. Xiaomi sought to become a leader in technology by consistently pushing the envelope and launching ground-breaking features. Xiaomi's brand identity was shaped by innovations like bezel-less displays, AI-driven cameras, and 5G connectivity, which also helped set it apart from rivals.

To meet the needs of different consumer demographics, Chew's market strategy employed a sophisticated method of client segmentation. Xiaomi's product line was created with a variety of market niches in mind, including luxury users, tech aficionados, and consumers on a tight budget. Xiaomi was able to provide solutions that were specifically matched to each target group's needs and preferences thanks to this segmentation strategy.

To take into account local tastes and market dynamics, Xiaomi's consumer segmentation also incorporated regional adaptation. Chew's approach comprised product and marketing customization for various geographies, accounting for cultural variances, varying levels of purchasing power, and advancements in technology. For instance, Xiaomi launched product versions and features that are suited to local requirements, like software that is customized and language options.

Given the substantial growth potential and need for reasonably priced technologies in emerging markets, Xiaomi gave these areas top priority. Chew's plan includes focusing on markets where Xiaomi could take advantage of its value proposition namely, India, Southeast Asia, and Latin America to gain market share. In these quickly expanding countries, the company concentrated on meeting the needs of cost-conscious consumers by providing premium items at low costs.

Xiaomi's aggressive pricing strategy was a pillar of the company's competitive strategy under Chew's direction. Xiaomi was able to obtain a competitive advantage by providing high-performance goods at a lesser cost than its rivals. Xiaomi's cost-cutting initiatives, direct-to-consumer sales approach, and effective supply chain management all backed this pricing strategy.

# Shou Zi Chew: Architect of the New Tech Era

Chew stressed the significance of ongoing product innovation to keep a competitive edge. Xiaomi made significant R&D investments to provide cutting-edge features that differentiate its devices from those of rivals. Xiaomi's competitive differentiation strategy was centered around innovations like AI-driven capabilities, high-resolution cameras, and improved display technology.

A combination of aggressive marketing, strategic alliances, and locally relevant tactics comprised Xiaomi's market penetration strategy. The company's attempts to increase its market presence by forming alliances with regional distributors, retailers, and e-commerce platforms were directed under Chew's leadership. Xiaomi expanded its reach and awareness in important markets by utilizing these alliances.

The placement of Xiaomi in the market was greatly influenced by its digital and e-commerce strategy. Chew's management concentrated on using Internet sales methods to contact customers directly, cutting out

Shou Zi Chew: Architect of the New Tech Era

traditional retail middlemen. Xiaomi was able to keep control over the customer experience, provide competitive pricing, and obtain insightful data about consumer behavior by adopting a direct-to-consumer strategy.

Xiaomi placed a significant focus on online marketing and social media interaction in its digital strategy. Chew's strategy included using digital channels to increase sales, interact with consumers, and raise brand awareness. To reach a wide audience and market its products, Xiaomi used influencer relationships, social media campaigns, and targeted web advertising.

Xiaomi maintains an omnichannel presence with physical retail outlets and experience centers in addition to its online sales approach. Chew's approach comprised opening Mi Stores and authorized service facilities to improve client interaction and offer hands-on experiences with Xiaomi goods. Xiaomi was able to offer a smooth shopping experience and accommodate a

## Shou Zi Chew: Architect of the New Tech Era

wide range of customer preferences thanks to its omnichannel strategy.

As part of its market positioning strategy, Chew established strategic alliances with leading companies in the sector and technology suppliers. These alliances made it easier to create cutting-edge technologies and integrations. For example, software developers and semiconductor makers worked together to create cutting-edge processors and to improve user experiences. Xiaomi was able to keep its competitive edge and add the newest advancements to its products by utilizing these relationships.

To increase market reach, Xiaomi's expansion plan includes forging agreements with distributors and retailers. Chew employed a strategy that involved forming partnerships with prominent retail chains, e-commerce platforms, and local distributors to guarantee the extensive accessibility of Xiaomi's merchandise. Through these partnerships, Xiaomi was

## Shou Zi Chew: Architect of the New Tech Era

able to expand into new markets, raise awareness of its brand, and boost sales.

To improve its market standing, Xiaomi entered into industry collaborations in addition to technology and retail alliances. Chew's approach comprised attending technological conferences, industry gatherings, and cooperative research projects. Through these partnerships, Xiaomi was able to present its inventions, connect with other companies in the field, and keep up with new developments.

To enhance Xiaomi's reputation and identity, Chew's market strategy placed a strong emphasis on brand building. This required making investments in sponsorships, public relations campaigns, and brand awareness activities. To stand out from rivals and forge a close bond with customers, Xiaomi sought to develop a good brand image linked to innovation, quality, and value.

## Shou Zi Chew: Architect of the New Tech Era

Xiaomi's market strategy placed a strong emphasis on increasing customer interaction and cultivating loyalty. As part of Chew's strategy, initiatives and programs were put in place to promote enduring customer relationships. Personalized discounts, special product releases, and loyalty programs were some examples of this. By interacting with consumers and offering outstanding support, Xiaomi sought to create enduring brand advocacy and loyalty.

An integral part of Chew's plan was creating a thriving community around Xiaomi's ecosystem and products. Through social media groups, development platforms, and online forums, Xiaomi promoted user communities. Users might exchange experiences, contribute feedback, and work together on product development in these communities. Xiaomi sought to strengthen brand loyalty and foster a feeling of community by supporting these communities.

Chew's approach to the market comprised monitoring new developments in the industry and modifying

## Shou Zi Chew: Architect of the New Tech Era

Xiaomi's product line appropriately. This involved keeping an eye on changes in consumer tastes, market dynamics, and technology improvements. Xiaomi was able to remain relevant and satisfy changing customer demands because of its rapid adaptation to these developments.

Chew's plan involved incorporating these ideas into Xiaomi's business procedures as consumers' concerns about sustainability and social responsibility grew. This included creating environmentally friendly goods, putting into practice sustainable production techniques, and lending assistance to charitable causes. Xiaomi sought to improve its market positioning and draw in socially concerned customers by tackling environmental and social issues and harmonizing with consumer values.

Future growth and innovation were given long-term attention in Chew's strategy plan. Setting high standards for market growth, technological innovation, and worldwide leadership was part of this. Xiaomi's long-term goal was to establish itself as a technological

## Shou Zi Chew: Architect of the New Tech Era

innovator by consistently pushing the envelope of innovation and providing customers with value.

Gaining worldwide market leadership was a major component of Chew's long-term plan. This entailed strengthening Xiaomi's brand recognition, growing the company's footprint in important overseas markets, and utilizing technology breakthroughs to spur growth. To position Xiaomi as a major force in the world of technology, Chew carried out a strategic plan that took into account both short- and long-term goals.

The market positioning and strategy of Shou Zi Chew have been essential in determining Xiaomi's success and worldwide reach. His all-encompassing strategy included consumer segmentation, competitive differentiation, digital and e-commerce tactics, brand building, and brand positioning. Xiaomi has grown significantly and become a major technology business under Chew's leadership by tackling a variety of market challenges and adjusting to new trends. In a market that is fiercely competitive and changing quickly, Xiaomi's market

Shou Zi Chew: Architect of the New Tech Era

positioning has been greatly aided by his strategic vision and execution.

## CHAPTER 4: CHALLENGES AND CONTROVERSIES

While Shou Zi Chew's leadership at Xiaomi has yielded many noteworthy successes, it has also required negotiating several intricate and varied hurdles. These difficulties have put the business's resiliency and strategic flexibility to the test, necessitating creative problem-solving and tactical changes on the part of Chew.

The main obstacles Xiaomi experienced during Chew's leadership can be divided into many important categories, including supply chain disruptions, regulatory obstacles, market competitiveness, brand reputation management, technology risks, and changing consumer tastes.

Xiaomi has had to contend with fierce rivalry from both up-and-coming and well-established tech companies in several different markets, including wearables,

## Shou Zi Chew: Architect of the New Tech Era

smartphones, and smart homes. Competitors with distinct advantages in terms of technological innovation, brand loyalty, and market presence, including Apple, Samsung, and Huawei, have presented serious obstacles. Chew used aggressive pricing, ongoing product innovation, and a commitment to providing customers with greater value as part of their approach to overcoming this obstacle. Despite these initiatives, Xiaomi's competitive advantage required constant strategy adaptation.

Businesses have aggressively lowered prices in an attempt to increase market share, a phenomenon frequently brought on by the fierce competition in the technology sector. Xiaomi, a company renowned for its value for money, has had to tread carefully in this market to keep its profit margins intact and appeal to consumers who are price conscious. Under Chew's direction, long-term growth and profitability were balanced with competitive pricing.

## Shou Zi Chew: Architect of the New Tech Era

As the technology industry develops, it is getting harder to distinguish Xiaomi's products from those of rivals. Xiaomi has had to come up with unique ways to differentiate itself from the various firms that are offering comparable features and technologies. To establish a distinctive market position, Chew focused on cutting-edge technology, distinctive features, and interconnected ecosystems. However, maintaining a clear differentiation requires ongoing effort.

Xiaomi has faced numerous difficulties as a result of geopolitical conflicts, mainly those that exist between the United States and China. Tariffs and trade disputes have hindered the company's capacity to conduct business as usual in important international markets. Chew's tactical approach involved broadening Xiaomi's supply network and investigating novel markets to alleviate the consequences of geopolitical unpredictability.

## Shou Zi Chew: Architect of the New Tech Era

Xiaomi has had to navigate complicated international trade restrictions and adjust its worldwide strategy in response to the changing political scene.

As a result of geopolitical considerations, Xiaomi has come under heightened regulatory scrutiny in several nations. For example, the business has had difficulties with data privacy laws and national security issues in countries like the United States and India. Chew's strategy included addressing issues in close collaboration with regulatory bodies, guaranteeing adherence to regional laws, and controlling possible risks related to global operations.

In some areas, geopolitical tensions have also resulted in limitations on market access. To sustain its global footprint, Xiaomi has had to modify its market entry methods and look into other avenues. In order to mitigate the effects of market limitations, Chew's leadership concentrated on forging solid local alliances and making use of area possibilities.

## Shou Zi Chew: Architect of the New Tech Era

Several events, including the COVID-19 pandemic, natural disasters, and geopolitical tensions, have caused major disruptions to the global supply chain. The inability of Xiaomi to get components, produce goods, and adhere to delivery schedules has been impacted by these disruptions. To lessen the effects of supply chain disruptions, Chew responded by diversifying its supply chain, adopting alternate sourcing tactics, and building up inventory levels.

Production capacity and product availability have been impacted by the technology industry's recent lack of vital components, such as semiconductors. Xiaomi has had to work with suppliers to manage these shortages by establishing trusting bonds, looking into new sources, and modifying production schedules. Chew's plan involved strengthening the supply chain's resilience and looking into vertical integration possibilities to gain access to crucial parts.

## Shou Zi Chew: Architect of the New Tech Era

Xiaomi has also faced difficulties as a result of disruptions in its distribution and logistics networks. The company's capacity to distribute goods effectively has been hampered by shipping delays and rising transportation expenses. Under Chew's leadership, supply chain visibility and efficiency were increased by using technology, investigating alternate distribution methods, and streamlining logistics operations.

Operating in a variety of international markets necessitates adhering to several local rules and regulations, such as those about consumer protection, product safety standards, and data protection. Xiaomi has had to overcome regulatory obstacles in several nations, which has required rigorous legal framework navigation and local requirement adaption. To guarantee compliance and proactively handle any regulatory problems, Chew's plan involved collaborating with legal and regulatory professionals.

Xiaomi and other tech businesses have raised serious concerns about data privacy and security. The business's

## Shou Zi Chew: Architect of the New Tech Era

procedures for gathering, storing, and using data have come under investigation. To solve privacy issues and win over customers, Chew's strategy included bolstering data security protocols, improving openness, and interacting with regulatory bodies.

Xiaomi has run into issues with rivals and patent holders on intellectual property. The company's capacity to develop and commercialize certain innovations has been hampered by the legal and financial difficulties these disagreements have caused. To lessen the burden of IP conflicts, Chew's approach included investigating licensing agreements, searching out peaceful remedies, and investing in intellectual property management.

Xiaomi has been the target of criticism and unfavorable press on several topics, such as the caliber of its products, privacy issues with data, and unfair business methods. Chew has had significant challenges in managing its brand reputation, which calls for proactive marketing initiatives and consumer interaction. The corporation has made an effort to improve customer service, increase product quality, and communicate openly to counteract bad press.

It has been difficult to maintain high standards of customer satisfaction and to efficiently handle consumer feedback. Under Chew's direction, customer support channels were strengthened, feedback mechanisms were put in place, and product support was enhanced. Xiaomi sought to develop a favorable brand reputation and encourage customer loyalty by responding to customer complaints and improving the overall customer experience.

Xiaomi has experienced quality problems and product recalls, which have damaged consumer confidence and the company's reputation. Chew's approach comprised putting strict quality control procedures in place, responding quickly to product problems, and being open and honest with impacted customers. The company's commitment to enhancing the quality and dependability of its products was crucial to preserving its strong brand image.

## Shou Zi Chew: Architect of the New Tech Era

Changing trends and quick technical breakthroughs define the technology sector. To be competitive, Xiaomi has had to keep up with technical advancements. Chew's strategy involved funding R&D, encouraging creativity, and modifying product plans to make use of new technologies. Overcoming the rapid advancement of technology and guaranteeing prompt product upgrades have proven to be constant obstacles.

Given its background in technology, Xiaomi has had to deal with dangers associated with hacking attempts and data breaches. Strong cybersecurity safeguards have proven essential for safeguarding private data and preserving customer confidence. Chew's approach comprised making investments in cybersecurity infrastructure, carrying out recurring security audits, and putting best practices for data security into effect.

It can be difficult to protect intellectual property and promote innovation while controlling related risks. Xiaomi has had to deal with issues with technology theft

Shou Zi Chew: Architect of the New Tech Era

and patent violation. Under Chew's direction, the company's discoveries were protected by bolstering intellectual property laws, funding R&D, and taking legal action where required.

In the tech sector, consumer expectations and tastes are always changing. Xiaomi has had to adjust to shifts in customer preferences, including a greater need for advanced features, personalized experiences, and sustainable products. Chew's approach comprised keeping an eye on consumer trends, gathering market data, and incorporating input from users into the creation of new products.

To adapt to changing consumer demands, Xiaomi has had to expand the range of products it offers. This has included looking into chances for innovation in already-existing product categories as well as branching out into new ones like electric cars and smart home technology. Under Chew's leadership, efforts to diversify were balanced with preserving the company's core competencies and brand identity.

## Shou Zi Chew: Architect of the New Tech Era

It has been difficult to satisfy customer demands for cutting-edge innovations while maintaining usability and practicality. Xiaomi has had to strike a balance between introducing cutting-edge technologies and taking user experience and practicality into account. Chew's approach comprised applying customer feedback to product creation, carrying out extensive market research, and emphasizing user-centric design.

Although Xiaomi's aggressive pricing policy has helped the company gain market share, it has also made it more difficult to continue operating at a profit. Growth and profitability have to be balanced, which has meant strict cost and financial control. Chew's strategy comprised expense control, income stream exploration, and operational efficiency optimization to guarantee long-term financial stability.

It has proven difficult to manage R&D, market expansion, and infrastructure investments while guaranteeing efficient resource allocation. Chew's approach comprised ranking high-impact investments in order of importance, evaluating market prospects, and matching resource allocation to strategic objectives. Achieving long-term goals and bolstering expansion plans have required effective financial management.

Xiaomi's financial performance has been impacted by various economic fluctuations and uncertainties, including fluctuations in currency exchange rates and global economic downturns. Under Chew's direction, risk management plans were put into practice, revenue streams were diversified, and economic conditions were adjusted to lessen the impact of financial uncertainty.

Throughout his time at Xiaomi, Shou Zi Chew has had to navigate a challenging array of situations, including competitive markets, geopolitical tensions, supply chain disruptions, legal obstacles, managing brand reputation, technology risks, changing consumer tastes, and financial management. Effective leadership, creative problem-solving, and strategic flexibility have all been necessary to meet these obstacles. Chew's capacity to handle these obstacles has been essential to Xiaomi's expansion, preservation of its competitive advantage, and setting up the business for long-term success in a dynamic and quickly changing international market.

## Major Decisions and Reactions

Shou Zi Chew has led Xiaomi through several contentious moves that have generated discussion and close examination. These choices have included everything from corporate policy and worldwide expansion initiatives to pricing and product strategies. With every dispute, Xiaomi has faced new difficulties that have called for calculated reactions to allay stakeholder worries and reduce possible dangers.

Xiaomi has drawn criticism and acclaim for its aggressive pricing approach, which entails selling

## Shou Zi Chew: Architect of the New Tech Era

premium technology products for much less than rivals. On the one hand, Xiaomi has been able to attract budget-conscious customers and gain a sizable market share thanks to this approach. However, it has given rise to charges of undercutting rivals and undervaluing tech-related goods.

Xiaomi has justified its pricing policy by emphasizing its dedication to offering cost-effective solutions and upending established pricing conventions. The company claims that it can offer affordable costs without sacrificing quality because of its direct-to-consumer sales approach, cost-effective supply chain, and emphasis on Internet marketing. According to Chew, Xiaomi's strategy aims to increase market competitiveness, open up access to cutting-edge technology, and spur innovation.

Xiaomi has been the target of complaints over data security and privacy, including issues with the way the firm collects and handles user data. Concerns over data security and privacy have been raised by reports that

# Shou Zi Chew: Architect of the New Tech Era

suggest Xiaomi's smartphones acquired sensitive user data and transmitted it to servers in China.

In response to this, Xiaomi has addressed privacy concerns in several ways in response to these accusations. The business has reaffirmed in public remarks its dedication to consumer privacy and data protection. Additionally, Xiaomi has taken steps to improve data protection, such as updating its privacy rules, being more open about how it handles data, and making an attempt to abide by international data protection laws. Chew's leadership has been crucial in resolving these issues by interacting with authorities and allocating funds for improvements in cybersecurity.

Xiaomi and its rivals have engaged in several patent and intellectual property (IP) battles. The main issue in these court cases has been accusations of patent infringement, with businesses saying Xiaomi's products infringed upon their rights to intellectual property.

## Shou Zi Chew: Architect of the New Tech Era

Xiaomi has taken a comprehensive legal approach to resolve these disputes. To settle disputes amicably, the business has negotiated and held settlement talks with patent holders. Investing in its intellectual property portfolio has helped Xiaomi fortify its position and safeguard its ideas. Xiaomi has improved its intellectual property management procedures and, where needed, has taken legal action to defend its technological innovations under Chew's direction.

Due to Xiaomi's quick international market expansion, there have occasionally been disputes over regional laws and business practices. For instance, because of compliance problems and regional regulatory requirements, the corporation has encountered regulatory hurdles and attention in markets including the United States and India.

In response to these controversies, Xiaomi has cultivated close relationships with local regulatory bodies to guarantee adherence to legislation relevant to the market. The corporation has modified product features, complied with local regulations, and improved its attempts to comply with regulations as part of its changes to business operations. Under Chew's direction, Xiaomi has had to navigate challenging regulatory frameworks and modify its business plans to suit the needs of various markets.

Xiaomi has been under fire for its products' poor quality, which has included product recalls and quality issues. Problems like flaws, errors, and inconsistent performance have affected how customers see a brand and its reputation.

Xiaomi has put in place strict quality control procedures and set up procedures for handling product recalls in response to concerns about the quality of its products. The business has made improvements to its quality assurance procedures, such as tighter quality checks and testing. Chew's leadership has included aggressive customer communication, open management of product problems, and initiatives to raise the general caliber and dependability of the product line.

## Shou Zi Chew: Architect of the New Tech Era

Xiaomi has been under fire for its sustainability initiatives and environmental policies. The usage of non-recyclable materials and the effects of Xiaomi's goods on the environment, particularly e-waste, has drawn criticism.

To allay these worries, Xiaomi has implemented several sustainability measures, such as enhancing the environmental impact of its operations and product development. The business has implemented eco-friendly materials, recycling initiatives, and sustainability objectives. Under Chew's direction, Xiaomi has emphasized its CSR efforts and endeavored to harmonize its operations with international sustainability norms.

There have occasionally been disagreements about Xiaomi's approach to PR and media scrutiny. The business has come under fire for how it has handled press coverage and public disputes, with some accusing it of being opaque and censoring information.

## Shou Zi Chew: Architect of the New Tech Era

By interacting with the media more proactively and directly addressing public issues, Xiaomi has worked to strengthen its media and PR strategy. The organization has made an effort to strengthen its rapport with media outlets, increase openness, and deliver precise and timely information. Under Chew's direction, communication plans have been monitored to control public opinion and properly handle media attention.

Xiaomi has occasionally caused investors to express worries about its strategic choices, particularly how it approaches product development, market expansion, and financial management. Investor confidence has been impacted by variations in profitability and market performance.

By emphasizing strategic financial management, enhancing operational effectiveness, and outlining its long-term objectives, Xiaomi has allayed investor fears. The business has made an effort to answer questions from investors, give clear financial reporting, and show

## Shou Zi Chew: Architect of the New Tech Era

that it is dedicated to long-term growth. Chew's leadership has been crucial in managing investor relations and guaranteeing that financial performance and strategic choices are in sync.

Xiaomi has been embroiled in a dispute with its marketing claims, which include allegations that it exaggerates the capabilities of its products or uses deceptive language in its advertising.

To ensure accuracy and compliance with advertising rules, Xiaomi has changed its advertising materials and modified its marketing methods in response to these incidents. The business has prioritized open communication and giving customers precise information about the capabilities and characteristics of its products. Under Chew's direction, marketing plans have been monitored and promotional activities have been made sure to comply with customer expectations and ethical standards.

Shou Zi Chew: Architect of the New Tech Era

Xiaomi has come under fire for its treatment of workers and the state of the workplace in its manufacturing plants, among other labor-related issues.

Xiaomi has improved working conditions and labor practices in response to these complaints. The organization has taken steps to improve worker welfare, guarantee equitable treatment, and adhere to labor laws. Under Chew's direction, labor-related concerns have been publicly addressed, and efforts have been made to promote a happy workplace.

Xiaomi has occasionally encountered disputes and conflicts with partners or stakeholders as part of its strategic relationships and collaborations.

To address these controversies, Xiaomi has held open discussions with partners, looked for win-win solutions, and made necessary adjustments to its strategic plan. The business has made an effort to keep good ties with important partners and make sure that joint ventures support its overarching strategic goals. Under Chew's direction, partnership dynamics have been controlled and disagreements have been resolved amicably.

Xiaomi has encountered challenges in corporate ethics and decision-making procedures, among other ethical dilemmas and governance issues.

Xiaomi has made efforts to fortify its ethical standards and corporate governance procedures to solve these problems. The organization has put policies and processes in place to guarantee moral behavior, openness, and responsibility. Under Chew's direction, the organization has a culture of honesty and ethical behavior that he has overseen and encouraged.

Over his time at Xiaomi, Shou Zi Chew has had to navigate several contentious choices and reactions. Pricing strategies, data privacy, intellectual property conflicts, market expansion, product quality, sustainability, public relations, investor relations, marketing methods, labor concerns, strategic partnerships, and corporate governance are just a few of

Shou Zi Chew: Architect of the New Tech Era

the topics that have been the subject of these controversies.

Every obstacle has needed careful and calculated replies, and Chew's leadership has been instrumental in resolving challenges, putting solutions in place, and guiding Xiaomi through challenging and dynamic situations. For Xiaomi to continue growing and succeeding, it has been crucial to handle and respond to these scandals well to preserve stakeholder trust and build the company's reputation.

## Key components of Shou's leadership

Taking A Look Back Throughout his time as Xiaomi's CEO, Shou Zi Chew has shared a plethora of knowledge and advice that can help enterprises and leaders navigate the challenging terrain of international technology markets. These lessons cover a wide range of organizational, operational, and strategic topics and

## Shou Zi Chew: Architect of the New Tech Era

highlight the possibilities and problems Xiaomi encountered under Chew's direction.

A key takeaway from Chew's leadership style is strategic agility's paramount significance. Rapid shifts in customer preferences, technical breakthroughs, and competitive dynamics characterize the technology industry. For Xiaomi to stay relevant and maintain a competitive edge, it has been crucial that it responds swiftly to these changes, whether by changing business models, investigating new markets, or refining product strategy. To be able to react quickly to new trends and unanticipated obstacles, leaders in their organizations need to foster an agile culture.

Chew's ability to adapt to shifting market conditions and unpredictabilities in geopolitics highlights the importance of having this flexibility. A strict strategy can impede growth, as Xiaomi's approach to expanding into new markets, changing pricing tactics, and diversifying its product line illustrates. Organizations should instead

# Shou Zi Chew: Architect of the New Tech Era

adopt a flexible strategy framework that enables quick modifications in response to evolving conditions.

Xiaomi's ability to strike a balance between innovation and cost efficiency has frequently been the key to its success. Under Chew's leadership, value was delivered and costs were properly managed while navigating competitive constraints. In a market where customers demand cutting-edge technology at affordable costs, striking this balance is essential.

To sustain profitability and market dominance, businesses need to engage in innovation in addition to putting effective operating procedures into place.

Another lesson is the necessity of comprehending and foreseeing competitive dynamics. Xiaomi has demonstrated a thorough awareness of rival strategies and market positioning through its strategic actions, which include aggressive pricing and technology developments. To stay ahead of the curve and make informed strategic decisions, leaders need to constantly analyze market trends and rivals.

Chew's experience emphasizes how crucial it is to comprehend and maneuver through intricate regulatory contexts. Business operations can be greatly impacted by national legislation and geopolitical issues. Proactively interacting with regulatory bodies, making sure local laws are followed, and anticipating regulatory changes that may impact their international operations are all necessary for successful firms.

Xiaomi offers a useful lesson in risk management through its methods of diversifying supply chains and looking into alternate markets to lessen the impact of geopolitical issues. Businesses should devise plans to lessen their dependency on any one market or supplier, which will lessen the possible effects of geopolitical unrest.

The significance of establishing trust via openness is emphasized by the lessons learned from Xiaomi's data privacy issues. Concerns over the collection and use of consumer data are growing. Chew has demonstrated via his leadership in improving data security safeguards and communicating with consumers that it is imperative to handle privacy concerns head-on to retain customer confidence and loyalty.

One important takeaway is the necessity of strong cybersecurity defenses. Technology businesses must invest heavily in cutting-edge cybersecurity processes and equipment as the threats posed by cyberattacks and data breaches continue to escalate. Protecting user data must be an organization's top priority, and to keep up with new threats, security procedures must be updated often.

Xiaomi's history of quality problems and product recalls highlights the need for a strong dedication to quality assurance. Reliability and performance criteria must be met by products to preserve customer satisfaction and brand reputation. Chew emphasizes the significance of placing a high priority on product quality throughout the

## Shou Zi Chew: Architect of the New Tech Era

whole manufacturing and design process by emphasizing the improvement of quality control procedures and open communication in handling product difficulties.

Proactive issue management is another topic covered in this course. Minimizing negative effects on the brand requires addressing possible quality issues before they become more serious and having efficient procedures in place for handling product recalls. Businesses should put strict testing procedures into place and create backup strategies for managing issues with quality.

Chew's management places a strong emphasis on the value of creating an organizational culture that is both flexible and resilient. It is essential to have a staff that is flexible, driven, and able to adapt to changes in a fast-paced sector. It is imperative for leaders to prioritize the establishment of a constructive work atmosphere, offer avenues for career advancement, and cultivate a climate of cooperation and creativity.

Shou Zi Chew: Architect of the New Tech Era

Two important takeaways from Chew's term are effective leadership and communication. Having open lines of communication with stakeholders, customers, and staff promotes alignment with corporate objectives and fosters trust. Leaders must possess transparency, approachability, and the ability to lead their teams through times of transition and uncertainty.

Xiaomi offers a useful lesson in sustainable development strategies with their strategy to strike a balance between ambitious growth and profitability. Although market share can be gained through quick expansion, it is crucial to make sure that growth is supported by profitable operations and good financial management. While pursuing development prospects, leaders should concentrate on creating strategies that promote long-term financial health.

Another lesson is how crucial it is to make thoughtful investment choices. Chew's handling of Xiaomi's capital expenditures in infrastructure, technology, and market expansion highlights the importance of prudent resource allocation and planning. Investments with the potential for significant returns and alignment with an organization's strategic goals should be given top priority.

Xiaomi's difficulties with media and public relations highlight the need for good reputation management. Leaders need to be ready to respond positively to both public criticism and media attention. Managing a brand's reputation and handling possible problems requires open communication, prompt replies, and proactive interaction with stakeholders.

Constant work is needed to create and preserve a positive brand image. Chew's emphasis on enhancing customer experience, resolving quality concerns, and interacting with customers emphasizes the necessity of continual efforts to improve brand perception. Businesses ought to fund projects that strengthen their brand values and establish a close rapport with their target market.

Shou Zi Chew: Architect of the New Tech Era

Strong IP management is crucial, as demonstrated by the lessons Xiaomi's intellectual property issues have taught us. A proactive approach to IP strategy and legal compliance is necessary to protect intellectual property and handle legal difficulties. Leaders ought to make investments in securing their discoveries, pursuing peaceful conflict settlement, and developing a robust portfolio of intellectual property.

Chew's experience highlights the importance of moral governance and decision-making. Establishing unambiguous ethical standards, encouraging an integrity-driven culture, and making sure that decision-making procedures follow moral principles are all necessary for organizations. Resolving moral conundrums openly and responsibly is crucial to the credibility and confidence of an organization.

One of the most important lessons from Xiaomi's success is the value of R&D investments. Maintaining a competitive edge in the technology industry requires constant technological innovation. Chew emphasizes the

## Shou Zi Chew: Architect of the New Tech Era

necessity for businesses to pursue innovation and make investments in cutting-edge technologies through his focus on R&D and technical breakthroughs.

Another important lesson is to welcome and adjust to technological change. Organizations need to be ready to adapt to new trends and embrace new technologies because the technology environment is always changing. Leaders must cultivate an innovative culture and guarantee that their establishments are adequately prepared to use technology breakthroughs.

The leadership of Xiaomi's Shou Zi Chew has offered a multitude of perspectives and lessons in company strategy and management. The insights gained provide invaluable direction for leaders and companies functioning in dynamic and intricate situations, covering topics such as managing geopolitical risks, addressing data privacy concerns, and the significance of strategic agility in handling competitive pressures. Businesses can improve their operational procedures, bolster their strategic approaches, and achieve sustainable success in

Shou Zi Chew: Architect of the New Tech Era

a constantly changing global market by putting these principles into practice.

# CHAPTER 5: PUBLIC AND INDUSTRY PERCEPTION

Any successful international technology business must consider media and public image. Shou Zi Chew's time at Xiaomi has been greatly impacted by these elements. A combination of the company's responses to outside scrutiny, controversies, and strategic decisions has defined Xiaomi's public image and media coverage. The way Xiaomi interacts with the media and the steps it takes to control its reputation offer a thorough case study of contemporary corporate communications.

A variety of media outlets, such as technology blogs, mainstream news, financial media, and social media platforms, cover Xiaomi in the media. The company has been highlighted in local and international media, demonstrating both its widespread reach and the wide range of interests held by various audiences. Product launches, company announcements, scandals, and regulatory difficulties have all been covered. The variety

## Shou Zi Chew: Architect of the New Tech Era

of media outlets that cover Xiaomi demonstrates the company's wide-ranging influence and the range of viewpoints that shape public opinion.

News reports, feature articles, opinion pieces, and reviews are just a few of the content kinds that have been covered by the media about Xiaomi. Major business announcements, such as the launch of a new product or a strategic plan, are frequently the subject of news headlines. Detailed analyses of Xiaomi's business tactics, competitive positioning, and technology advancements are presented in feature articles.

Opinion articles and editorials present personal opinions about the company's actions and effects. these opinions are frequently shaped by larger trends in the industry and societal issues. Customer perceptions are shaped by reviews, especially those of Xiaomi's devices, which emphasize technology innovations and user experiences

Xiaomi's public perception has been significantly influenced by its product innovations and debuts. The

## Shou Zi Chew: Architect of the New Tech Era

company has received a lot of media attention for its strategy of providing premium technology at affordable costs. Xiaomi's value proposition, design aesthetics, and technology innovations are frequently emphasized in product reviews and feature stories. Good press surrounding the launch of new products can improve Xiaomi's standing as a creative and customer-focused company.

Xiaomi has been the subject of several controversies and criticisms, which have been reflected in media coverage. There has been a lot of coverage of topics like intellectual property disputes, data privacy concerns, and poor product quality. Unfavorable public impression in these areas might result in scrutiny from industry watchers, regulators, and consumers. The way Xiaomi handles and reacts to these issues is very important in determining how the public perceives the company.

Xiaomi's public perception has been greatly impacted by its dealings with regulatory bodies and legal issues. The company's reputation may be impacted by media

# Shou Zi Chew: Architect of the New Tech Era

coverage of regulatory challenges, such as those involving data privacy or adhering to local laws. Reporting about legal conflicts, notably those involving intellectual property, affects investors and the general public's perception of the company.

To control its public image, Xiaomi has used proactive media relations techniques. Press releases, media gatherings, and interactions with journalists to share details and perspectives about the business are all examples of this. Xiaomi seeks to ensure accurate depiction and a positive impact on media coverage by actively crafting the narrative surrounding its products and efforts.

Transparent communication and prompt responses to media requests are essential for managing media scrutiny effectively. Xiaomi has had to deal with several issues relating to media attention, and part of its strategy has been to personally address complaints, offer clarifications, and rectify disinformation. This proactive strategy aids in controlling any possible harm to the company's reputation.

To improve its reputation, Xiaomi has also made use of media partnerships. Working together with media outlets, industry experts, and technology influencers can help you reach specific audiences and magnify good press. Xiaomi can shape how the media views its brand and products by cultivating relationships with important media stakeholders

Keeping a good public image requires effective crisis management. Xiaomi takes a quick response, open communication, and practical problem-solving strategy while managing emergencies. For instance, Xiaomi has shown a dedication to problem-solving by keeping customers informed about corrective efforts, communicating directly with them in the event of product recalls or quality issues, and providing updates. By using this strategy, the company's reputational harm is lessened and stakeholder trust is restored.

# Shou Zi Chew: Architect of the New Tech Era

A crucial facet of Xiaomi's PR approach is cultivating brand loyalty. The company has concentrated on giving customers satisfying experiences by offering premium goods, prompt customer support, and interesting marketing initiatives. A positive public image and long-term loyalty are fostered by positive consumer interactions and a strong brand presence.

Xiaomi's CSR(Corporate Social Responsibility)programs have a big impact on how people perceive the company. The business has supported education efforts, promoted sustainability, and assisted with community development, among other social and environmental projects.

Xiaomi's adherence to social responsibility is emphasized by media coverage of these initiatives, which also helps to strengthen Xiaomi's standing as a conscientious corporate citizen.

Constructively resolving criticisms and implementing corrective action in areas of concern are key components

## Shou Zi Chew: Architect of the New Tech Era

of managing bad media coverage. In response to the many comments it has received, Xiaomi has acknowledged problems, made adjustments, and shared advancements. Xiaomi wants to show its commitment to ongoing improvement and accountability by confronting bad media head-on.

Highlighting the company's accomplishments and successes contributes to the maintenance of a favorable public perception. Through media attention and PR campaigns, Xiaomi has emphasized its technology advancements, market successes, and consumer pleasure. Public opinion is strengthened and a favorable brand narrative is added by showcasing these accomplishments.

One of the most crucial parts of controlling brand perception is having direct interactions with customers via forums, social media, and other platforms. These channels have been used by Xiaomi to communicate with customers, respond to issues, and get input. Interacting with customers fosters goodwill, allows you

## Shou Zi Chew: Architect of the New Tech Era

to quickly resolve problems, and shows that you are attentive to their needs.

The public perception of Xiaomi has been greatly influenced by social media. Social media sites like Facebook, Instagram, and Twitter offer avenues for direct communication with customers and larger audiences. Social media posts that are both positive and negative can affect media attention and public opinion.

Keeping an eye on discussions, reacting to user comments, and resolving issues are all part of managing a social media presence. Xiaomi has promoted products, managed brand reputation, and engaged in direct consumer communication via social media. Good social media management contributes to influencing public opinion and enabling prompt responses to new problems.

Xiaomi's public perception may be impacted by user-generated material, such as social media posts, reviews, and testimonials. Good user-generated content can boost a business's reputation and offer sincere recommendations for its goods. On the other hand, unfavorable content might draw attention to possible problems and shape public opinion. Xiaomi's strategy involves responding to user issues and promoting great user experiences.

Public opinion of Xiaomi's goods is greatly influenced by product reviews. While bad reviews can draw attention to possible problems and harm a brand's reputation, positive evaluations can increase customer confidence and drive sales. To properly manage public opinion, Xiaomi responds to product reviews by addressing feedback, making improvements, and communicating updates.

Broader market trends and industry advancements have an impact on media coverage as well. The competitive environment, market dynamics, and Xiaomi's positioning within the technology industry all influence the company's public perception. Xiaomi can adjust to changing market conditions and preserve a positive public image by keeping up with industry changes and modifying its strategies accordingly.

Xiaomi's public perception is greatly influenced by transparency and accountability. The organization works to foster trust with stakeholders and customers by being upfront about its policies, addressing problems transparently, and exhibiting accountability. An organization's reputation can be preserved by responding to difficulties and effectively communicating business policies.

Strategic preparation and constant work are necessary to create and maintain a positive public image. Xiaomi's reputation has been shaped throughout time by its emphasis on innovation, customer satisfaction, and corporate responsibility. Maintaining transparency and fulfilling brand commitments regularly contribute to a positive reputation over time.

As consumer choices, market dynamics, and media coverage change over time, so too can public perception.

Shou Zi Chew: Architect of the New Tech Era

To keep its good reputation, Xiaomi must be able to adjust to shifting public opinion and resolve new issues. With constant customer interaction, media attention, and feedback, Xiaomi can efficiently manage changing perceptions.

Creating a positive public perception requires effective strategic communication and brand management. Xiaomi's strategy entails managing media relations, interacting with stakeholders, and meticulously developing messages. Xiaomi may impact public opinion and improve its reputation by putting into practice a strategic communication plan and concentrating on brand management.

The success of a technology business is greatly influenced by media coverage and public perception, as Shou Zi Chew's stint at Xiaomi has demonstrated. Xiaomi offers important insights into successful corporate communications with its approach to media coverage and public image, from handling disputes and managing media relations to cultivating brand loyalty

Shou Zi Chew: Architect of the New Tech Era

and interacting with customers. The takeaways from Xiaomi's experiences highlight the value of strategic adaptability, open communication, and proactive involvement in upholding a favorable public perception and negotiating the intricate terrain of international technology marketplaces.

## Industry Opinions and Critiques

These are crucial in determining how the general public views technology businesses, how confident investors are, and how consumers make decisions. Under the direction of Shou Zi Chew, Xiaomi has attracted a diverse array of viewpoints and criticisms from media pundits, industry analysts, and technological specialists.

These viewpoints shed light on Xiaomi's commercial tactics, placement in the market, and general influence on the technology industry.

## Shou Zi Chew: Architect of the New Tech Era

Xiaomi's inventiveness and technological breakthroughs have earned it widespread recognition. The company has been commended by industry observers for its capacity to provide superior technologies at affordable costs. One of Xiaomi's main competitive advantages is the way it incorporates cutting-edge technologies into its products, like fast charging capabilities, sophisticated camera systems, and connections with smart homes.

Industry observers frequently point to Xiaomi's dedication to innovation as the cause of the company's explosive expansion and market share. Although Xiaomi is a creative company, some have questioned the novelty of its technological innovations. Concerns have been expressed by certain industry insiders over the company's preference for using and improving upon already-existing technologies over creating brand-new ones. Opponents contend that although Xiaomi is excellent at implementing ideas at a low cost, it might be slow to develop innovative technologies that have the potential to revolutionize the market.

## Shou Zi Chew: Architect of the New Tech Era

Customers and industry experts alike have shown a great deal of support for Xiaomi's aggressive pricing strategy. Analysts applaud the startup for questioning established pricing structures and opening up cutting-edge technologies to a wider market. This strategy is thought to be a disruptive force in the industry, making rivals reevaluate their value propositions and price plans

Opinions in the industry frequently emphasize Xiaomi's accomplishment in using its economical supply chain to provide high-quality goods at reduced costs. On the other hand, Xiaomi's price model has drawn criticism for not being sustainable. A few industry watchers are worried that the company's low-margin strategy would not hold up over time.

There are worries that the unwavering emphasis on keeping costs low may hurt profitability and make it more difficult to scale operations or make investments in new technologies in the future. The aggressive pricing of technology products has drawn criticism for perhaps undermining their perceived worth and fueling price wars that could damage the market as a whole.

Industry insiders have generally backed Xiaomi's attempts to strengthen its data protection procedures in the wake of security and privacy-related scandals. The company's efforts to increase openness, update privacy policies, and fund cybersecurity measures have been recognized by analysts.

Proactively tackling privacy problems is perceived favorably and as an essential step towards rebuilding customer confidence and adhering to global data protection regulations. Some detractors of Xiaomi's data management methods continue to harbor doubts despite these initiatives. There are still worries over the volume of data being collected and the possibility of data breaches.

With concerns about digital privacy growing, industry observers have questioned whether Xiaomi's data protection safeguards are adequate. To make sure that the

## Shou Zi Chew: Architect of the New Tech Era

business's data practices comply with legal obligations and best practices, there is a push for stricter standards and impartial audits.

Business analysts have commended Xiaomi for its audacity and strategic vision in its audacious plan to expand globally. The company's efforts to establish a foothold in regions including Southeast Asia, Latin America, and Europe, along with its diversification into new markets, have been viewed as examples of a well-executed expansion plan.

Analysts frequently point to Xiaomi's success abroad as largely attributable to its capacity to customize its goods and promotional tactics to regional tastes. Xiaomi's international growth hasn't been without controversy, especially in light of its lack of flexibility in response to shifting laws and market dynamics. Opponents have highlighted difficulties in adhering to regional laws, including those about trade prohibitions and data privacy.

Shou Zi Chew: Architect of the New Tech Era

There are worries that Xiaomi's quick growth can result in operational inefficiencies or make it more challenging to handle a convoluted international supply chain. A few industry watchers also wonder if the company's aggressive strategies for breaking into new markets will cause problems with local partners or government agencies.

Industry experts who understand the value of preserving ideas have endorsed Xiaomi's efforts to defend its intellectual property and resolve patent disputes. It is believed that the company's aggressive strategy of developing a strong intellectual property portfolio and taking legal action to defend its patents is essential to preserving its competitive edge and promoting innovation.

Despite this, Xiaomi's participation in IP litigation has drawn criticism. Several industry watchers fear that the business's ongoing legal battles could take funds away from innovation and harm its reputation. Prolonged legal action, according to critics, may give the impression that

## Shou Zi Chew: Architect of the New Tech Era

a company is aggressive and could damage ties with other tech companies. A more cooperative strategy for managing intellectual property is being called for, one that puts industry collaboration ahead of court cases.

Industry observers have given Xiaomi's corporate social responsibility initiatives which include community assistance programs and environmental sustainability initiatives a favorable rating. The corporation is viewed as taking action to solve environmental issues and improve its social effect by investing in sustainable practices like cutting down on e-waste and using eco-friendly materials.

Analysts frequently point to Xiaomi's CSR initiatives as a crucial component of the company's overall business plan and brand image. Nevertheless, Xiaomi has come under fire for the size and efficacy of its CSR campaigns. Given the size of its operations and the environmental impact of manufacturing technologies, several industry analysts wonder if the corporation is making enough environmental efforts.

## Shou Zi Chew: Architect of the New Tech Era

More thorough and open reporting on sustainability objectives and results is demanded. Additionally, detractors call on Xiaomi to move more vehemently to accomplish its long-term social and environmental goals.

It is commonly known that Xiaomi's emphasis on providing premium goods at reasonable costs is a strength. Reviews from the industry frequently laud the business for providing a strong value proposition, with items that blend cutting-edge technology with affordable prices. Positive consumer comments and satisfaction with Xiaomi's product performance and overall quality are often highlighted by analysts.

Notwithstanding these advantages, uncertainties exist over the uniformity of product excellence. Certain devices have been criticized for having flaws and dependability problems, which has led some critics to question Xiaomi's quality control procedures. The corporation is being urged to improve its quality assurance procedures to guarantee that all of its goods

## Shou Zi Chew: Architect of the New Tech Era

fulfill rigorous requirements and function consistently. Resolving these issues is essential to preserving consumer confidence and enduring brand allegiance.

Xiaomi's public relations tactics and marketing initiatives, together with its overall brand management approach, have been acknowledged for their success in creating a powerful brand presence. The company's ability to craft an engaging brand narrative and interact with customers through a variety of channels is frequently praised by industry experts. A positive brand image and strong consumer attachment can be attributed to the emphasis on innovation and value for money.

Xiaomi's response to a few PR emergencies has drawn criticism, nevertheless. Commentators in the business have questioned the company's handling of unfavorable press coverage and customer grievances. Sustaining a positive public perception requires effective crisis management, and there have been requests for Xiaomi to improve its methods for dealing with problems openly and quickly.

## Shou Zi Chew: Architect of the New Tech Era

Investors and analysts have given Xiaomi's financial performance—including its revenue growth and market share expansion—positive recognition. The company's capacity to grow significantly in a cutthroat market is thought to be evidence of its effective business plans and positioning in the marketplace.

Notwithstanding its robust expansion, Xiaomi's sustained profitability remains a matter of concern. Regarding the company's potential to maintain good profit margins while adhering to an aggressive price policy, several analysts are skeptical. It's been discussed that Xiaomi needs to strike a balance between profitability and expansion to maintain long-term financial stability and investor confidence.

Views from the industry and criticisms of Xiaomi under Shou Zi Chew's direction offer a thorough understanding of the company's advantages, disadvantages, and opportunities for development. Although Xiaomi has received praise for its inventiveness, price policy, and

## Shou Zi Chew: Architect of the New Tech Era

international growth, it has also been under fire for issues with data privacy, intellectual property rights, and product quality.

As Xiaomi continues to negotiate the challenging terrain of the technology business, it will be imperative that it responds to these criticisms and capitalizes on encouraging comments from the community. Through prioritizing openness, improving product quality, and striking a balance between expansion and profitability, Xiaomi can endeavor to uphold a favorable public perception and attain enduring prosperity in the worldwide marketplace.

# CHAPTER 6: PERSONAL INSIGHT AND PHILOSOPHY

At Xiaomi, Shou Zi Chew's management style and leadership style offer a special fusion of operational effectiveness, strategic vision, and adaptable leadership. His emphasis on innovation, international growth, and skillful handling of both internal and external obstacles have characterized his time as CEO.

Xiaomi wants to become the world leader in technology, and Chew's leadership is typified by a long-term strategic vision towards this end. This ambition includes growing Xiaomi's market share as well as promoting technological innovation and creating fresh business strategies. Chew's strategic vision has directed Xiaomi's product line expansion, technological adoption, and entry into a variety of markets. His capacity to foresee

## Shou Zi Chew: Architect of the New Tech Era

market changes and match Xiaomi's strategy with new prospects has been crucial to the success of the business.

Chew places a high priority on innovation, which is fundamental to his leadership style. Under his direction, Xiaomi has concentrated on pushing the boundaries of technology and incorporating state-of-the-art components into its devices. Chew has supported programs that encourage teams to try out novel concepts and push the limits of technical advancement to cultivate an innovative culture within the organization. This innovative strategy has enabled Xiaomi to stand out in the technology industry and preserve its competitive advantage.

Data-driven decision-making plays a major role in Chew's management style. He has underlined how crucial it is to use analytics and data to guide operational and strategic decisions. Through the examination of customer behavior, market trends, and performance measures, Chew and his team have made well-informed decisions that have boosted business growth and improved operational efficiency. Xiaomi has been able to enhance its product development procedures, manage its supply chain, and boost its marketing efforts thanks to this data-centric approach.

Chew's management approach is centered on operational effectiveness. He has put in place methods and procedures meant to increase efficiency, cut expenses, and boost overall performance. Xiaomi places a strong emphasis on efficiency across all facets of its operations, including customer service, transportation, and manufacturing. Chew's focus on process efficiency and cost control has helped Xiaomi continue to be profitable while providing premium goods at competitive costs.

Chew's leadership style is distinguished by a calculated approach to international growth. Acknowledging the prospects for expansion in global marketplaces, Chew has led initiatives to solidify Xiaomi's foothold in other territories. In addition to entering new countries, Xiaomi's worldwide development plan entails customizing its goods and business methods to suit

## Shou Zi Chew: Architect of the New Tech Era

regional tastes and legal requirements. Xiaomi's successful worldwide expansion has been largely attributed to Chew's ability to negotiate a variety of market situations and cultivate partnerships with local partners.

A crucial component of Chew's management strategy is market adaptation. He has underlined how crucial it is to comprehend regional variations and modify Xiaomi's offerings and promotional tactics to suit regional demands. This entails modifying price plans, personalizing product attributes, and interacting with regional customers through focused advertising. Xiaomi has developed a strong worldwide brand and gained popularity in a variety of areas thanks to Chew's emphasis on market adaption.

Chew places a high priority on encouraging a collaborative work atmosphere and giving people a sense of empowerment. He is an advocate of giving team members responsibility and letting them take charge of their work. Chew has established a work climate that

## Shou Zi Chew: Architect of the New Tech Era

provides resources and support while granting autonomy, resulting in motivated and respected people. This empowerment has helped Xiaomi foster an innovative and high-achieving culture.

Chew's management style places a strong emphasis on collaboration. He has encouraged open communication between several departments and cross-functional teamwork. This cooperative setting fosters idea exchange improves problem-solving skills and promotes group achievement. Chew's emphasis on teamwork has enabled Xiaomi to accomplish its objectives and overcome obstacles by utilizing a variety of viewpoints and areas of expertise.

Chew's leadership has been put to the test by several crises, such as problems with products and regulations. He uses open communication and proactive tactics in his crisis management strategy. Chew has shown tenacity and dedication to upholding Xiaomi's image by confronting problems head-on and taking appropriate

Shou Zi Chew: Architect of the New Tech Era

action. His adept handling of crises has enabled Xiaomi to weather difficult times and come out stronger.

Developing organizational resilience is a key component of Chew's management strategy. This entails getting ready for the business to adjust to shifting conditions and bounce back from failures. Chew has put tactics into place to improve Xiaomi's adaptability and agility, enabling the business to act quickly in the face of unforeseen difficulties and market shifts. For Xiaomi to be sustainable and successful over the long run, resilience building has been essential.

Chew's leadership style is based mostly on a customer-centric mindset. His emphasis on the value of comprehending and satisfying consumer wants is evident in Xiaomi's approach to product development and marketing. Through the prioritization of client feedback and its integration into the design of products and services, Chew has made sure that Xiaomi's offerings are in line with what customers anticipate. Xiaomi has been

## Shou Zi Chew: Architect of the New Tech Era

able to increase consumer happiness and brand loyalty by putting a heavy emphasis on the customer experience.

Chew has also supported efforts that aim to have direct contact with customers. This entails using social media, polling customers, and attending business gatherings. Xiaomi learns a great deal about the preferences and worries of its customers through active customer engagement, which helps with product development and marketing tactics. Chew's focus on customer involvement has improved Xiaomi's entire market presence and audience relationship.

A key component of Chew's management philosophy is ethical leadership. He has stressed how crucial it is to uphold strict moral principles and cultivate an integrity-focused culture at Xiaomi. This entails following legal standards, guaranteeing open company procedures, and encouraging moral conduct among employees. Chew's dedication to moral leadership contributes to the development of stakeholder trust and upholds Xiaomi's standing as an ethical business.

## Shou Zi Chew: Architect of the New Tech Era

To guarantee efficient supervision and accountability, Chew's approach to corporate governance involves putting in place strong regulations and procedures. This entails creating transparent governance frameworks, keeping an eye on legal compliance, and managing any hazards. Sustaining stakeholder relationships, preserving investor trust, and assuring the organization's long-term performance all depend on strong corporate governance.

Long-term growth and strategic goal-setting are key components of Chew's outlook for Xiaomi's future. This entails creating creative business strategies, investing in cutting-edge technologies, and investigating new markets. Xiaomi is guaranteed to stay competitive and well-positioned for future success thanks to Chew's forward-thinking strategy. Chew hopes to sustain Xiaomi's leadership in the technology industry and promote sustainable growth by regularly assessing market trends and modifying tactics.

Shou Zi Chew: Architect of the New Tech Era

Looking ahead, Chew has placed a heavy emphasis on these two areas. This entails tackling social and environmental issues, developing technical innovation, and incorporating sustainable practices into daily operations. Chew's emphasis on sustainability indicates a dedication to making a beneficial effect while promoting economic success and is in line with larger industry trends.

At Xiaomi, Shou Zi Chew's management style and leadership style are a culmination of a sophisticated fusion of operational effectiveness, strategic vision, and adaptable leadership. His focus on innovation, international growth, and customer-focused tactiles has been crucial to Xiaomi's development and success. Through the use of excellent crisis management, team empowerment, and adherence to moral principles, Chew has transformed Xiaomi into a robust and adaptable entity. His innovative strategy and dedication to sustainability set Xiaomi up for long-term success in the rapidly changing technology sector.

Shou Zi Chew: Architect of the New Tech Era

## personal convictions

An in-depth understanding of the reasons and self-reflections behind a person's professional path and leadership style is possible through these sources. Shou Zi Chew's approach to leading Xiaomi and negotiating the challenging technology landscape has been greatly inspired by his personal views and motivations. His goals, experiences, and personal values provide a thorough awareness of the elements influencing his leadership and decision-making.

Shou Zi Chew's early experiences in his career and educational background have greatly influenced the way he approaches life and his goals in the workplace. His education at prominent colleges like University College London and Harvard Business School gave him a strong background in technology and business. His analytical and strategic thinking were refined by these formative

## Shou Zi Chew: Architect of the New Tech Era

experiences, which also ingrained in him a dedication to excellence and lifelong learning. Chew's broad viewpoint and leadership style are a result of his early exposure to a variety of academic subjects and work settings.

Chew's leadership style is heavily influenced by his values, which include honesty, tenacity, and a dedication to innovation. His upbringing in Singapore and exposure to many cultural settings have shaped his outlook on life and method of doing business. The significance of moral behavior, long-term planning, and a commitment to providing value to stakeholders are all emphasized by Chew's ideals. His decision-making processes are guided by these principles, which also influence how he interacts with partners, customers, and coworkers.

Chew's leadership at Xiaomi and career decisions are motivated by his enthusiasm for technology and creativity. His work path has been guided by his desire to be at the forefront of technological developments and shape the future of technology. Chew's focus on product development and strategy choices reflects his passion for innovation, problem-solving, and new technology exploration. His ambition to head an organization at the forefront of technical advancement is fueled by this devotion.

Chew's dedication to using technology to improve the world is a major source of motivation. His motivation stems from the chance to develop goods and services that enhance people's lives and deal with social issues. Chew's leadership at Xiaomi is indicative of a larger desire to have a significant impact, be it via improving community development, advancing sustainability, or improving connectivity. His corporate activities and strategic priorities are guided by his unwavering dedication to leveraging technology for positive purposes.

From his observations, Chew reveals a philosophy of leadership that combines practical application with forward-thinking ideation. He understands how critical it is to have a clear strategic direction while maintaining

## Shou Zi Chew: Architect of the New Tech Era

flexibility in response to shifting conditions. Chew is a leader who places a strong emphasis on empowering colleagues, promoting cooperation, and stimulating creativity. His observations frequently emphasize striking a balance between addressing pressing operational issues and upholding a long-term goal. This strategy demonstrates a thorough comprehension of the challenges involved in running a multinational technology business.

Looking back on his experiences, Chew has discovered important managerial and leadership skills. He understands the value of forging strong bonds with stakeholders, the necessity of ongoing learning, and the significance of resilience in overcoming obstacles. Chew's observations highlight how important flexibility, empathy, and strategic thinking are to good leadership. His approach to managing Xiaomi and navigating the ever-changing technology market has been shaped by these lessons.

Shou Zi Chew: Architect of the New Tech Era

Chew wants to have a big influence on the world technology market, which is why he is spearheading Xiaomi's international expansion. The task of making Xiaomi a household name worldwide and growing its presence in new markets drives him. In addition to expanding Xiaomi's market share, Chew sees Xiaomi as a worldwide leader that pushes innovation and establishes new benchmarks for the sector. His desire to succeed in the long run and leave a lasting impact on the technology industry is evident in this goal.

Chew is driven to answer practical issues and improve user experiences, which is why he is concentrating on consumer-centric innovation. Creating products that appeal to customers and offer real advantages is what motivates him. Understanding customer preferences, taking feedback into account, and providing solutions that address changing demands are all priorities for Chew's leadership. A fundamental component of his motivation and strategic goal for Xiaomi is this customer-centric approach.

## Shou Zi Chew: Architect of the New Tech Era

Chew's introspective thoughts on adversity demonstrate a tenacious and resilient core. He accepts the challenges and disappointments he has faced during his career and sees them as chances for development. Chew's tenacity and problem-solving abilities are demonstrated by his ability to handle market issues, handle crises, and get around regulatory obstacles. His observations emphasize the value of keeping an optimistic outlook, adjusting tactics, and overcoming obstacles.

Chew utilizes his leadership of Xiaomi's teams as part of his approach to fostering resilience, which goes beyond his own experiences. His drive stems from the desire to establish a work atmosphere where staff members are equipped to overcome obstacles and prosper in changing circumstances. Chew's leadership places a strong emphasis on building and assisting teams as well as cultivating a cooperative and flexible culture. His views on resilience highlight the significance of building a solid organizational culture and equipping teams to handle ambiguity.

## Shou Zi Chew: Architect of the New Tech Era

Chew wants to push technological breakthroughs that will change the sector and enhance people's lives. This is reflected in his vision for the future of technology. The opportunity to develop new technologies, investigate cutting-edge trends, and spearhead innovation in the technology industry excites him. Chew is dedicated to keeping on the cutting edge of technical advancement and helping to shape the direction of technology, which is part of his forward-looking perspective.

Chew expresses a wish to be recognized for having had a significant and enduring influence on the technology sector in his comments on his legacy. His legacy is one of creativity, leadership, and corporate social responsibility. Chew's drive to establish a robust and long-lasting business is a reflection of his dedication to generating value for stakeholders, advancing technology, and enhancing social well-being.

One of Chew's main driving forces is his fervent belief in corporate social responsibility (CSR). His motivation stems from his conviction that technology businesses

## Shou Zi Chew: Architect of the New Tech Era

ought to make a positive impact on society and the environment. Chew is a leader at Xiaomi who prioritizes ethical behavior, community involvement, and sustainability. His reasons for getting involved in CSR are part of a larger goal to match corporate success with beneficial societal impact.

Chew is driven by the chance to interact with and assist communities via Xiaomi's CSR programs. His introspective writings highlight the significance of tackling environmental and social issues as well as promoting community growth. Xiaomi's initiatives to boost social welfare, encourage environmental sustainability, and support education are examples of Chew's dedication to corporate social responsibility.

Chew acknowledges the significance of preserving well-being and personal fulfillment in his comments on striking a balance between work and personal life. He understands the pressures of a prominent leadership position and the necessity of skillfully handling stress and obligations. Chew prioritizes spending time with

## Shou Zi Chew: Architect of the New Tech Era

family, pursuing hobbies, and making sure that job obligations don't take precedence over personal well-being when it comes to work-life balance.

A key component of Chew's leadership is his dedication to upholding moral principles and honesty in his work life. Honesty, accountability, and respect are among his basic beliefs, and he makes an effort to match his judgments and behaviors with these ideals. Chew's contemplations emphasize the significance of adhering to ethical norms and personal values while managing the challenges of a leadership position.

The motivations and introspection of Shou Zi Chew provide insightful information on the principles that guide his managerial and leadership style. His early influences, career goals, dedication to social responsibility and innovation, and leadership style all shaped Xiaomi's strategic direction. Chew's contemplations on surmounting obstacles, cultivating adaptability, and harmonizing personal and professional spheres highlight his unwavering commitment to leaving

Shou Zi Chew: Architect of the New Tech Era

a lasting impression and attaining sustained prosperity. Xiaomi's success and global positioning can be attributed to the leadership of the company, which is guided by his own goals and ideals.

## CHAPTER 7: FUTURE OUTLOOK

A time of rapid development and innovation at Xiaomi has been ushered in under Shou Zi Chew's leadership, and the business has several prospective projects and objectives that could significantly impact its future course. These programs are in line with Xiaomi's strategic goal, which aims to improve its market position, advance technology, and cater to changing customer demands. This thorough summary explores Xiaomi's upcoming initiatives and goals under Chew's direction, emphasizing their importance and possible effects.

Given the significant development potential in emerging regions, one of Xiaomi's main objectives is to establish a strong presence in these areas. With customized approaches, the organization hopes to expand into areas including Southeast Asia, Latin America, and Africa. This entails presenting its current product selection in addition to creating solutions tailored to the demands and preferences of the local market. Chew's leadership underscores the significance of comprehending regional subtleties and forming robust local alliances to proficiently manage these heterogeneous markets.

Xiaomi intends to make investments in localized product development to facilitate this expansion. This includes developing gadgets that cater to particular needs and tastes that are particular to these areas, like features that are regional, durable, and affordable. For example, the business is looking into ways to improve energy-efficient technology and connectivity solutions that fit the infrastructure needs of developing nations. Chew's strategy goal is to make sure Xiaomi's goods are affordable and appealing to local customers.

A key component of Xiaomi's technological strategy is the company's emphasis on advances in machine learning (ML) and artificial intelligence (AI). Future initiatives will incorporate AI into a range of product categories, including wearables, smartphones, and smart home appliances. By implementing clever features like sophisticated picture analysis, personalized recommendations, and natural voice interactions, the aim is to improve user experiences. Chew envisions using AI to provide more adaptive and seamless technological solutions that enhance daily living.

Xiaomi is increasing its capacity for AI research and development (R&D) to facilitate these advancements. This entails founding brand-new R&D facilities and working with top universities and research groups. The company wants to push machine learning advances, investigate new applications, and enhance its AI technologies. Chew is committed to making sure Xiaomi stays at the forefront of AI research and can effectively integrate these developments into useful products for consumers.

Xiaomi is pursuing several green technology projects as part of its dedication to environmental sustainability. The goal of these initiatives is to lessen the company's operations and product's environmental impact. Enhancing the recyclability of materials used in Xiaomi's products, cutting down on electronic waste, and

## Shou Zi Chew: Architect of the New Tech Era

increasing energy efficiency are among the main objectives. Chew's leadership is committed to incorporating sustainable practices at every stage of the supply chain, from production to disposal at the end of product life.

Xiaomi intends to expand its operational usage of renewable energy sources. This involves making investments in wind and solar energy to run its corporate offices and manufacturing facilities. The business is also looking into how to create products and technologies that are less energy-intensive and have a smaller carbon footprint. Chew wants to establish Xiaomi as a pioneer in environmentally friendly technology, taking into account changing consumer demands and wider market trends.

With the addition of new smart home technologies and linked gadgets, Xiaomi's IoT ecosystem is expected to grow. Future initiatives will focus on creating smart home items that are easier to use and more integrated than current Xiaomi models. The company wants to

Shou Zi Chew: Architect of the New Tech Era

improve consumer convenience and automation by developing a more unified and user-friendly IoT environment. Chew's plan calls for increasing device compatibility and diversifying the selection of smart home solutions.

Key breakthroughs in this area include developments in smart appliances, security systems, and energy management solutions. Xiaomi is working on building products that offer expanded functionality, such as smart energy monitoring, better security features, and integrated home control systems. Chew's leadership is geared toward making smart home technology more accessible and user-friendly, ultimately improving the quality of life for consumers.

Xiaomi is planning to launch a new generation of flagship smartphones with enhanced features and cutting-edge technology. These upcoming models are likely to contain advancements such as upgraded camera systems, higher processing rates, and enhanced connectivity options. Chew's strategic goal is to ensure

Shou Zi Chew: Architect of the New Tech Era

that Xiaomi's flagship smartphones continue to establish industry standards and deliver great performance.

The new smartphones will integrate the latest breakthroughs in technology, including 5G capability, augmented reality (AR), and enhanced battery life. Xiaomi is also researching the potential to add AI-driven features and increased security measures. Chew's focus is on retaining Xiaomi's competitive edge in the smartphone market by offering high-quality smartphones that match the increasing needs of consumers.

Xiaomi is investing in the expansion of its e-commerce platforms to boost its digital sales channels. Upcoming projects include improving the online purchasing experience, boosting digital marketing activities, and strengthening customer engagement through personalized content and recommendations. Chew's mission is to build a seamless and engaging e-commerce experience that promotes sales and strengthens customer relationships.

# Shou Zi Chew: Architect of the New Tech Era

The organization is also working on merging its digital platforms to deliver a more unified and integrated user experience. This involves making Xiaomi's web services, mobile apps, and digital content offerings more functional. Chew is strategically focused on using digital platforms to build an ecosystem that is more connected and supports Xiaomi's larger goals.

To promote growth and innovation, Xiaomi is constantly looking to form strategic alliances. These alliances could entail working together with leading technological firms, academic institutions, and businesses. The objective is to increase market prospects and speed up development by utilizing outside resources and experience. Strong, win-win alliances that support Xiaomi's strategic objectives are highly valued under Chew's leadership.

The expansion of Xiaomi's network of goods and services is another priority. This entails boosting interoperability, developing a more integrated user experience, and generating synergies across several product lines. According to Chew, Xiaomi's ecosystem

## Shou Zi Chew: Architect of the New Tech Era

will be expanded to include a wide range of linked goods and services that give customers more value.

Xiaomi places a high premium on improving the customer experience. Future initiatives will increase post-purchase assistance, expedite communication channels, and improve customer support services. Chew's management is committed to making sure Xiaomi offers top-notch customer care at all stages of the customer journey, from pre-purchase questions to post-purchase assistance.

To better serve each customer's demands, the organization is also attempting to provide more individualized services. This entails using analytics and data to offer personalized advice, made-to-order fixes, and proactive assistance. Chew wants to give customers a more tailored, responsive experience that fosters happiness and loyalty.

Xiaomi intends to add fresh, cutting-edge items to its line of wearable technology. It is anticipated that

## Shou Zi Chew: Architect of the New Tech Era

wearables in the future will feature improvements in fitness tracking, health monitoring, and connectivity with other Xiaomi devices. According to Chew, wearables should have more functionality, better accuracy, and seamless communication with Xiaomi's larger ecosystem.

Improving health and wellness features is one of the new wearables' main goals. This involves creating gadgets that assist training objectives, track a range of physiological factors, and offer thorough health insights. Chew wants to establish Xiaomi as a leader in wearable technology by offering goods that improve customers' quality of life in general.

To promote innovation and technical improvement, Xiaomi is dedicated to maintaining its investment in research and development (R&D). Plans call for building up R&D facilities, investing more in state-of-the-art technologies, and encouraging an innovative work environment within the organization. Under Chew's direction, Xiaomi can continue to grow and preserve its

## Shou Zi Chew: Architect of the New Tech Era

competitive advantage thanks to research and development.

To meet changing customer expectations and growing trends, the organization intends to investigate new technological frontiers and provide creative solutions. This involves making investments in fields like cutting-edge material science, quantum computing, and next-generation display technology. Chew wants to make sure Xiaomi keeps pushing the boundaries of technology innovation and producing ground-breaking goods and services.

Several ambitious forthcoming projects and strategic goals that demonstrate Xiaomi's dedication to expansion, innovation, and market leadership are indicative of Shou Zi Chew's leadership at the firm. Future initiatives from Xiaomi, such as breaking into emerging countries, developing AI technologies, improving sustainability, and creating next-generation devices, have the potential to make a big difference and change the course of the firm. Chew's strategy focuses on innovation that is

Shou Zi Chew: Architect of the New Tech Era

customer-centric, technological improvement and worldwide expansion highlighting his vision for Xiaomi's sustained success and leadership in the technology industry. These initiatives and objectives will be crucial in determining Xiaomi's future and solidifying its standing as a top global technology business as it develops.

## Future Forecasts for the Technology Sector

The technology sector is expected to undergo significant transformations in the upcoming years due to advances in multiple fields, changing consumer preferences, and new global issues.

It is anticipated that ML and AI will be progressively incorporated into commonplace services and applications. Automation, predictive analytics, and personalized experiences will all develop thanks to artificial intelligence (AI) in a variety of industries, including manufacturing, retail, healthcare, and finance. More advanced and precise applications will be made possible by improved AI algorithms and more potent computing resources, completely changing how companies function and engage with their customers.

As AI technology develops, regulatory frameworks and ethical issues will receive more attention. Concerns regarding algorithmic bias, data privacy, and transparency will bring up issues relating to responsible AI use. To guarantee that AI technologies are created and applied in ways that are morally and just, governments and organizations will endeavor to create policies and standards.

As 5G networks are deployed, faster data rates, reduced latency, and better connectivity will be experienced. This will make progress easier in fields like augmented reality (AR), smart cities, and the Internet of Things (IoT). 5G will facilitate the expansion of linked devices, open up new applications, and improve mobile experiences.

There will be a surge in the study and advancement of 6G technology. It is anticipated that 6G will provide significantly higher data speeds, extremely low latency, and more sophisticated features than 5G. Even though 6G adoption may not happen for years, these initial advancements will pave the path for later innovations and enhancements in communication and networking.

As businesses look to process data closer to their source to save bandwidth and latency, edge computing will become more popular. Businesses can enhance the performance of services and applications that need real-time data processing, like industrial automation, smart city infrastructure, and autonomous vehicles, by utilizing edge devices and local processing.

By allowing data to be handled locally as opposed to being sent to centralized cloud servers, edge computing will also solve security and privacy problems. This will improve data security and lower the possibility of data breaches, particularly for applications that need high-security levels and sensitive data.

As quantum hardware and algorithms progress, quantum computing is anticipated to reach important benchmarks. Drug discovery, encryption, and optimization difficulties are just a few of the difficult issues that quantum computers may be able to resolve. These issues are outside the purview of traditional computers. Advancements in this domain will propel novel scientific findings and breakthroughs.

Although large-scale, fault-tolerant quantum computers might still be in the works, efforts to market quantum computing technologies will likely increase. Applications for quantum computing will advance and become more widely available with the help of cloud-based quantum computing services and collaborations between tech businesses and academic institutes.

## Shou Zi Chew: Architect of the New Tech Era

As more devices get connected and able to communicate with one another, the Internet of Things ecosystem will keep growing. Innovations in data analytics, sensor technologies, and connection solutions will propel this expansion. Applications for the Internet of Things will include industrial sensors, environmental monitoring systems, wearable technologies, and smart household appliances.

To enable smooth communication between various IoT devices and platforms, interoperability and standards will be more important as the number of connected devices rises. Organizations and industry groupings will endeavor to create uniform frameworks and standards that will make it easier to integrate various IoT systems.

As these technologies advance, they will provide increasingly immersive and engaging experiences in AR and VR. The functionality and realism of AR and VR applications will be improved by advancements in software, content creation, and hardware, such as AR glasses and VR headsets.

## Shou Zi Chew: Architect of the New Tech Era

Entertainment, education, healthcare, and real estate are just a few of the fields in which AR and VR will find use. For instance, whereas VR will facilitate distant cooperation and virtual simulations, AR will be utilized for interactive teaching and education. These innovations will change how individuals engage with virtual worlds and interact with digital content.

As technology permeates more aspects of daily life, there will be a greater need than ever for effective cybersecurity defenses. Protecting sensitive data from online dangers like ransomware, phishing scams, and data breaches will become a top priority for both individuals and organizations. Protecting digital assets will need investments in cutting-edge cybersecurity technologies, threat detection, and incident response.

As governments impose more stringent guidelines to safeguard consumer data, data privacy laws will inevitably change. Businesses must abide by laws like the California Consumer Privacy Act (CCPA) and the

## Shou Zi Chew: Architect of the New Tech Era

General Data Protection Regulation (GDPR) to keep the trust of customers and stay out of trouble with the law.

As part of its commitment to environmental responsibility, the technology sector will place a greater emphasis on sustainability and green technologies. This entails creating goods that use less energy, cutting down on electronic waste, and implementing environmentally friendly production techniques. Businesses will make an effort to reduce their environmental effect and support international initiatives to tackle climate change.

The IT sector will adopt the circular economy concept, which emphasizes reusing, recycling, and cutting waste. Businesses will investigate strategies for creating longer-lasting products, putting take-back plans in place, and incorporating recycled materials into their supply chains. Technology's environmental impact will be lessened and more sustainable consumption patterns will be encouraged by the move towards circular economy models.

Shou Zi Chew: Architect of the New Tech Era

The workplace will continue to change as more and more people choose remote and hybrid work arrangements. Virtual workspaces, project management software, and video conferencing are just a few examples of the technologies that will continue to be crucial for remote communication. Businesses will spend money on digital tools and platforms that facilitate flexible work schedules and boost output.

Enhancing remote work environments and encouraging teamwork among dispersed teams will be the main goals of work technology innovations. This covers developments in digital employee engagement platforms, productivity solutions powered by AI, and virtual collaboration tools. Future workplaces will prioritize employee well-being, have more flexibility, and better communication.

Thanks to developments in genetics, customized medicine, and digital health solutions, biotechnology and health tech will witness breakthroughs. Advances in biotechnology will allow for more individualized healthcare planning, early disease detection, and more precise therapies. Expanding access to medical services and improving patient outcomes are two benefits of integrating technology into healthcare.

Wearable medical technology, telemedicine, and health monitoring applications are just a few examples of the rapidly developing digital health technologies. These developments will promote preventive health initiatives, improve remote treatment, and offer real-time health analytics. The emphasis on digital health will meet the rising need for easily available and effective medical treatments.

The technology sector is about to undergo a profound metamorphosis, as new developments and trends are poised to reshape several facets of everyday life and corporate operations. The digital world will continue to change quickly, from the increased use of AI and 5G to the expansion of IoT and the emergence of sustainable solutions. These forecasts demonstrate the industry's dynamic character as well as the chances and difficulties

## Shou Zi Chew: Architect of the New Tech Era

that lie ahead. Technology will have a significant impact on the future as it develops, fostering innovation, enhancing lives, and solving global issues.

Shou Zi Chew: Architect of the New Tech Era

# CONCLUSION

In "Shou Zi Chew: Architect of the New Tech Era," we have journeyed through the remarkable career of a visionary leader who has profoundly influenced the landscape of modern technology. From his early days in the tech industry to his transformative role at the helm of major digital platforms, Chew's strategic insights and innovative approaches have reshaped how we interact with technology. His tenure has been marked by a commitment to pushing boundaries and fostering growth, demonstrating the power of visionary leadership in navigating and shaping the digital age.

As we conclude, it is clear that Shou Zi Chew's impact extends beyond mere technological advancements. His work exemplifies how strategic foresight, adaptability, and a relentless pursuit of innovation can drive an era of unprecedented change. Chew's contributions are not just markers of success in the tech industry but also serve as

Shou Zi Chew: Architect of the New Tech Era

a blueprint for future leaders aspiring to navigate the complexities of the modern digital world. His journey underscores the importance of bold vision and thoughtful leadership in crafting the future of technology.